GLORIOUS ECCENTRICS

GLORIOUS ECCENTRICS
MODERNIST WOMEN PAINTING AND WRITING

Mary Ann Caws

GLORIOUS ECCENTRICS
© Mary Ann Caws, 2006.

First published in 2006 by
PALGRAVE MACMILLAN™
175 Fifth Avenue, New York, N.Y. 10010 and
Houndmills, Basingstoke, Hampshire, England RG21 6XS
Companies and representatives throughout the world.

PALGRAVE MACMILLAN is the global academic imprint of the Palgrave Macmillan division of St. Martin's Press, LLC and of Palgrave Macmillan Ltd. Macmillan® is a registered trademark in the United States, United Kingdom and other countries. Palgrave is a registered trademark in the European Union and other countries.

ISBN-13: 978–1–4039–6595–0
ISBN-10: 1–4039–6595–1

Library of Congress Cataloging-in-Publication Data

Caws, Mary Ann.
    Glorious eccentrics : modernist women painting and writing / Mary Ann Caws.
        p. cm.
    Includes bibliographical references and index.
    ISBN 1–4039–6595–1 (alk. paper)
        1. Women artists—History—19th century. 2. Women artists—History—20th century. 3. Women authors—History—19th century. 4. Women authors—History—20th century. I. Title.

N8354.C39 2006
700.92′2—dc22   2006042958

A catalogue record for this book is available from the British Library.

Design by Newgen Imaging Systems (P) Ltd., Chennai, India.

First edition: December 2006

10 9 8 7 6 5 4 3 2 1

Printed in the United States of America.

There is nothing so strong as growing.

—*Emily Carr,
journal of June 5, 1938*

Contents

Permissions

Dorothy Bussy:

Archives, Bibliothèque nationale. Dossier Roger Martin du Gard. By permission from Louis Lacroix and Caroline Saulses de Freycinet.

Excerpts from *Selected Letters of André Gide and Dorothy Bussy*. ed. Richard Tedeschi. Oxford and New York: Oxford University Press, 1983. By permission of Oxford University Press.

Claude Cahun:

Claude Cahun, *Ecrits*: édition présentée et établie par François Leperlier. Paris: Jean-Michel Place, 2002. By permission of Jean-Michel Place.

Claude Cahun Photographe, Exhibition Catalogue, Musée d'Art Moderne de la Ville de Paris. Paris: Jean-Michel Place, 1995.

Emily Carr:

Excerpts from *Hundreds and Thousands* by Emily Carr, from *The Complete Writings of Emily Carr*, published by Douglas & McIntyre Ltd. Text of *Hundreds and Thousands* Copyright © 1966 by John Inglis, Estate of Emily Carr. Reprinted by permission of the publisher.

Excerpts from *The Life of Emily Carr*. Copyright © 1987 by Paula Blanchard. Published by Douglas & McIntyre Ltd. Reprinted by permission of the publisher.

Excerpts from *Growing Pains: An Autobiography* by Emily Carr. Toronto: Irwin, 1946. Reprinted by permission of the publisher.

Shadbolt, Doris. *The Art of Emily Carr*. Seattle: University of Washington Press, 1979.

The Emily Carr Omnibus. Seattle: University of Washington Press, Shadbolt preface, 1993.

These seven stories illuminate some little-known
aspects of many famous men

Gerald Brenan
André Breton
Simon Bussy
Puvis de Chavannes
Edgar Degas
César Franck
Roger Martin du Gard
Théophile Gautier
André Gide
Victor Hugo
Leconte de Lisle
Pierre Loti
Pierre-Auguste Renoir
Toulouse-Lautrec
Henri Michaux
Ralph Partridge
Rainer Maria Rilke
Erik Satie
Lytton Strachey
Catulle Mendès
Maurice Utrillo
Richard Wagner

This is Personal

My Grandmother a Painter

Here is where it started, my book about these extraordinary women. At home.

Margaret Walthour Lippitt, my grandmother, never made a self-portrait. A painter of still lifes, mountain landscapes, and portraits, she never turned her artist's eye toward her own visage. I used to wonder what this meant, at a time when many women painters wanted to capture their own likeness—for themselves, for others, for posterity. Perhaps it had something to do with Southernness; I was never to know. Perhaps some sense of modesty. Perhaps it doesn't matter.

She rose early to paint, usually about five in the morning. For the rest of the day, unless she had a sitter for a portrait, she devoted herself to social necessities (calling, being called upon), and to cuisine, and to hospitality. She was a southerner to the hilt, given to generous reaching out, and, as sometimes happens, to the interior drive that can accompany it. So she had no time for regarding herself—that is most probably it, the reason I had been looking for.

Her great-grandfather had been president of the University of Alabama, and she was born in that state. She taught painting in the South, scooping up her hair into a bun and fastening glasses onto her nose, to look older than she was. She was quite early called to Washington, to entertain and receive for her uncle, Senator Henry Pugh, and wedded Devereux Haigh Lippitt, from Wilmington, North Carolina, who worked in cotton with William Walker and Lawrence Sprunt.

Then an extraordinary thing occurred. Grandmother left her year-old baby behind her, with the family doctor guaranteeing to look in on tiny Maxwell every day, when he was taken out for a walk, and betook herself to the Académie Julian in Paris. About that, she talked, but I didn't know yet how to listen.

Later, when a cotton exchange was being set up in Bremen, Germany, she of course accompanied her husband there. About sixteen miles to the north of Bremen, in a tiny rural town called Worpswede, was the art colony set up by Otto Modersohn, Hans von der Ende, and Franz Overbeck. There Grandmother felt at home. She knew the poet Rilke, and was a close friend of Otto Modersohn, about whom she sometimes spoke. She studied with Frank Duveneck, working in Munich, whose family was close to the Henry and William James family, and who had himself studied at the Académie Julian. Duveneck eventually moved back to America with his wife Lizzie Boott, also a painter, until her early death. A bronze replica of her memorial statue, surrounded by lilies, is in the American wing of New York's Metropolitan Museum.

The family returned to North Carolina at the outbreak of the war, when Grandmother's husband sent a wire in code saying it was "time to get tickets for the play." They left in haste. Grandmother studied first with Hans Hofmann in Provincetown and then with other teachers. All this time, she was painting and painting, as well as being a hostess and a mother; and she decided to give none of it up. This characteristic energy was accompanied by a parallel fascination by the smallest details: a sitter's high cheekbones, a special flower in a bouquet, or a splash of ochre. The names of colors she intoned for me—cadmium yellow, burnt siena, cornelian—stick in my mind, all as joyous. Her work exults in rich-textured brocades, purple eggplants, and green ginger jars—the same kind Cézanne so often included in his still lifes.

I wanted to celebrate, in an act of deeply and avowedly personal criticism, that fact of inseparability of intensities that I find glorious. When I wrote an impassioned book called *Women of Bloomsbury*, I tried to sketch the complicated interrelations of three women with each other and their work: Virginia Woolf, Vanessa Bell, and Dora Carrington. That I do not see their lives or art or deaths as tragic, despite the suicides of two of them and the trials all of them suffered, represents a kind of moral choice. I ended that book with a hope that the reader might feel, instead of an observer, before whose eyes an unusual life is performed like a drama, part of a family of concerned readers, the real audience I would like to be writing for. I dedicated that book to "my grandmother, who dared to be an artist," and who was, as I have said, at the origin of my present writing.

She never exhibited her paintings in her lifetime. Now they are shown here and there—in various museums and homes, where they are cherished with the same sort of intensity with which they were created. Over my sofa in Manhattan, an improbable place for it, I suppose, hangs my favorite, *A Cadet's Room*, from 1897, with its musical score, its enigmatic manuscript, and the cadet's sword, in glowing brownish colors. It lends to my smallish space all the past it can take in. Near it hangs a painting by Robert Vonnoh, Grandmother's best friend in Old Lyme, Connecticut, whose wife, Bessie Potter Vonnoh, was a sculptress, one of whose statues I enthroned above my bookcase. Others are in Brookgreen Gardens in South Carolina the park across from the Flower Hospital in New York, and on and on. How important these remembrances of Grandmother's life are to me—they bear a resonance far beyond themselves. I can hear the chimes of noon when I look at Vonnoh's painting, can hear Grandmother's voice telling me what books those are in the *Cadet's Room*, what musical score that is.

I have made my own collection besides: a strange and tall Vuillard, where a woman is disappearing into the righthand frame—reminding me of Mallarmé the ur-Symbolist and high priest of understatement, in whose texts and paintings, something seems always about to happen even as it disappears in the margins. Here is the figure leaving and all the more present, in her reddish cloak. Here are a few of Duncan Grant's portraits of Vanessa Bell, with their child, angelica, and as a painter, and a few of her own paintings, delicate still lifes, like his own—in flat bright colors. A charcoal drawing by Suzanne Valadon, with a nude fresh from her bath, sinuous standing beside her immense towel, reminds me of her red chalk drawings Degas hung on his wall. "You are one of us," he had said. Here is a Carrington, with a plunging perspective onto a table with peonies, and a drawing with the names of the colors to come sketched in. I love the idea that they are always to come.

As for my grandmother's daring, I didn't practice a lot of that, starting in the antique South draped with moss and manners. I wasn't like her when I was growing up. I didn't take the time to learn to paint, as she wanted me to. Not even to make a cake as she wanted to teach me. I didn't know how to listen, maybe not even how to look.

And still, here I am now, wanting to write about her. Comic as it sounds, the most modest art slide room moves me, as if it were a sacred place. I whisper; I get lost. "You don't have to whisper here," said an art historian friend of mine once to me. But I do, because it's the tangible link to my grandmother. I can feel her paintings living in me, smell the linseed oil she would wipe off on her smock, watch how the little spot of cadmium yellow she would put somewhere among the grey trees would illuminate the whole canvas, taste the hot tabasco in the thick black bean soup she would serve for special occasions and the straggly threads of fresh peaches in the ice cream she would make in between her long sessions in the studio.

In my apartment, sometimes now, standing between her painting and that of Carrington, I hold up one of her tiny Breton cups made in the 1890s, handpainted, even before they were numbered on the bottom, hold it hard to bring back that kind and wrinkled face and those sparkling eyes. I long just to have another chance to ask her what it was like then, now that I've learned to listen. I don't want it to be always too late, so I've made another start to my story of her story. I'm speaking to her: "It must have been different in the nineteenth century, when what you did had so much color to it," I say.

> You were so tall, you carried yourself like a model, your auburn hair was down to your waist. Like a Titian, they said at the Beaux-Arts — mother had told me this about you. "Auburn," the very name sounds magical to me, quite like Burnt Siena. How did you learn you were a painter? Did you just one day pick up a brush, or pencil, and sketch something out? Had someone found a drawing and exclaimed? How does it happen, that you find out who you are?

Maybe I'll find that out sometime, soon, or then later. I've made so many starts now to this old new story that is my life, but what I remember holds good. My grandmother taught me to be at ease in my drivenness, and stands for me as my mentor in work and living. So she begins this book, about a group of extraordinary women, painting, writing, photographing, and living—all of them with an energy characteristic of a certain eccentricity, as I see it. And them.

Why These Women

Many of us, readers of lives and texts, encountering such traces as letters and journals, share a biographer's fascination with how we might best plot a narration, chronological or thematic. What comes first, it seems to me, is the choice of the particular story we want to tell, of its characters as of its events. I have cared greatly about these strong lives. On the outermost level, these women represent several different nationalities: French, British, Canadian, German. Each of their stories has a definite strangeness to it, and is marked by a definite excess. Each character has her own obsessions, drama, and style. I find these women to be way out there, of great personal appeal, and gifted with a peculiar sort of endurance.

I'll begin with one dream told by Emily Carr, the Canadian painter and writer, comparable to Whitman in poetry close to the forests of the Northwest coast, whose epic she chose to paint. She dreamt it on April 15, 1934, and tells it in her journal of the next day:

> I woke to this dream: I was in a wood with lush grass underfoot and I was searching for primroses and a little boy came. I did not see him, only his bare feet and legs among the grass and I saw my own feet among the grass also. "What are you looking for?" said the boy. "Primroses." "There are no primroses here," said the boy, "but there are daisies. Gather them." Perhaps what I want most is not for me. I am to "gather daisies" instead of primroses. (Journals, 112)

I suppose that dream and its subsequent realization are about knowing what Carr calls elsewhere "the song of this place." Finding your own peculiar place and its tone, which might just not match your original idea about yourself. Trying to convey someone else's tone, song, and sense of place is a risky business: I can only hope I will be hearing the right sound for each of these creators I am choosing to speak of—it is that sound I have tried to capture and pass on.

In a sense, the choice by a painter or writer of her place, or her vision of a personal assignment to it, already motivates the self-portrait. Emily Carr writes, on the last day of 1940, "To write a self-portrait should teach one something about oneself. I shall try." (HT, 330) Each of these women attempts that kind of writing or painting or photography. Among the most memorable self-portraits are those of the young and beautiful Suzanne Valadon in 1883, with her gorgeous red hair, and at 65, in 1931, with her bare-breasted courage; of Paula Modersohn-Becker, with the amber beads around her neck, shortly before her early death; and of Claude Cahun in all her various self-portrait photographs, early to later, in her different garbs and masks and haircuts. And in the written portraits, the journals and letters of Judith Gautier, Dorothy Bussy, Emily Carr, Paula Modersohn-Becker, and Dora Carrington. We have a fine sense of all these extraordinary eccentrics, who may give us strength for our own individual ways of dealing with the world, ourselves, and our work.

Painting Women

A few years back, I published a paper called "Ladies Shot and Painted." It dealt with surrealist portraits and photographs of women, who were often personally involved with the painters and photographers, and who were quite often complicit with the sensuality of their rendering—like a kind of double gift, I maintained, to the artist and to us. In 1981, Rozsika Parker and Griselda Pollock collected their ideas on the topic, and, like the crucially important writings of Linda Nochlin, and of Whitney Chadwick, both of whom deal with the issues of women painters and power, their *Old Mistresses: Women, Art and Ideology* has been useful to all of us writing after.

They point out how unusual it was, in the late nineteenth century, for a woman of the class of Paula Modersohn-Becker to pursue a professional career instead of simply displaying her accomplishments. (*Old*, 108) One of the great heroines of the time, Marie Bashkirtseff, claimed loudly: "I am my own heroine. . . I am so peculiarly constituted that I regard my life as something apart from me and on that life I have fixed all my ambitions and hopes . . . ." "She continued: "there is nothing of the woman about me but the envelope." (*Old*, 109) In Modersohn-Becker's celebrated *Self-portrait Female Nuide*, the demonstration of her own identity as bare-breasted, and the natural setting, with her amber beads around her neck, are daring indeed, and show the influence of Gauguin, in particular of his 1890's portraits, such as *Tahitian Women with Mango Fruits* of 1899. In the tiny rural backwater of Worpswede, near the bustle of Bremen, her own class position and her allegiance to the time's "reactionary German ideologies about Earth, Nature, and Natural Woman. . . ." called a surprising attention to the possibility of new relationships between creativity and fecundity, seen as scandalous to those of her somewhat puritanical bourgeois background.

Suzanne Valadon, trapeze artist and artist's model—famous for her modeling of Renoir's *The Bathers* (the bather on the righthand side, with a pouting mouth and a retroussé nose)—before she became a painter and the mother of Maurice Utrillo, is perhaps the most scandalous of all. In her self-portrait of 1883, her assertive gaze challenges that of the observer. In her *Nu à la Palette* of 1927, she is sixty-five, and her baring of her breasts goes far past propriety's norms. By contrast, far more typical and less challenging is a painting like Matisse's 1917 *Painter and his Model*, in which the female model, lying back in the chair, is faceless, and the male artist, clothed, unlike Picasso's famous

Painter and his Model series. This is the placid assertion of masculinity to which the observer was accustomed. But the women painters in this book did much that was unaccustomed. My pages here want to serve as testimony to their work.

Note on the Biographical Elements in this Book

As will be instantly apparent, I regard the term "eccentric" as an approbation rather than a criticism, as the very opposite of pejorative. Given the unstandard nature of their lives, I have in no way wanted to write standard biographical portraits of these women, for most of whom such portraits already exist. So I will not be examining their youth or upbringing or schooling or even the influences on them of other writers and painters. My interest lies elsewhere.

Most appealing to me are the crucial moments of their lives or thoughts, those crisis points that mold the mind and heart and grip the imagination. I have chosen to speak of these women because their very intensity beckons my own—not the particulars of their lives, but the odd details that challenge society's norms and beckon to us others, eccentric in our own way, often interior.

Does one ever think of oneself as eccentric? Perhaps. My sense of the *interior eccentric*, to be considered alongside the more obvious exterior eccentric, derives from my reading of the literal dictionary sense of the word, that is, *ex-centric:* deviating from the center or the norm. It suggests a behavior inappropriate to the context of one's life or situation, to the specific social circumstances, a way of life or love or work deliberately chosen instead of given. Is there, I will be asked, something about being a woman that equips someone in some peculiar fashion for her surprising behavior? Is it something about her having to work against established preconceptions or traditional obstacles? Were I to answer in the affirmative, I would hasten to place Marcel Proust, Henry James, and Joseph Cornell—all three among my heroes—in their company. A supersensitive strain might be thought to elicit an intensity of emotion and reaction conducive to the creative intertwining of life and work illustrated here.

Each of these women was working against the more probable script preordained for her. This againstness is what best fit her for her own "selving," as Gerard Manley Hopkins would have said. Reading these lives and others of which they remind us, we each must draw our own conclusions about their sense of self, and ours.

ACKNOWLEDGEMENTS

I want particularly to thank the following:

The Bibliothèque Jacques Doucet in Paris; the archives of the Bibliothèque Nationale in Paris; the archives of the Fonds Masle in the Bibliothèque Kandinsky at the Musée National de l'Art Moderne; the archives of the Parnall Collection in Victoria, British Columbia; the Archives of the Harry Ransom Humanities Research Center, Austin, Texas.

The late Frances Partridge, for sharing with me her recollections of Carrington; the poet Adrienne Rich for permission to use her poem about Paula and Clara; and various friends and persons who helped in innumerable ways: Boyce Bennett, Hilary and Jonathan Caws-Elwitt; Matthew Caws, Linda and Arthur Collins, Marie-Claire and Maurice Dumas, Carolyn Gill, Peter Jones, Paula Kamenish, Ruth Middleton; Franck Perrussel, Adrienne Rich, Peg Rorison, Grace Schulman, Janet and Malcolm Swan, Lizzie Thymme, Sarah Bird Wright, Virginia Zabriskie, and my agent Katherine Fausset.

I owe a particular debt to the Rockefeller Foundation at Bellagio, for having offered me a place to write this, and friends with whom to discuss the notion of eccentricity and these representatives of it. Thank you all.

CHAPTER 1

JUDITH GAUTIER

ORIENTALIST MUSE

I am Chinese. . . . I shall be, all my life, a sort of Far-Eastern woman detached from her time and her setting.

> —*To Raoul Aubry, interview about being the first woman in the Académie Goncourt (Le Temps, Nov. 25, 1920, JR, 225)*

This book's first eccentric story is probably the most colorful. It was already odd from its beginning. In it and around it, Romanticism held sway. Judith Gautier was the daughter of Théophile Gautier and his long-standing mistress, the contralto Ernesta Grisi (cousin of the famous contralto Julia Grisi, and the elder sister of the famous dancer Carlotta, principal of Gautier's ballet *Giselle*, Carlotta whom Gautier adored). But his daughters—Judith did not find out for a long time that she had a sister, Estelle—came from the other one, Carlotta's elder sister.

Judith later wrote about her own reluctant birth:

> They tell me I showed a good deal of repugnance at coming into the world. . . . [H]aving been compelled to do so, I showed my displeasure with a real burst of anger; I screamed, and seized the doctor's fingers, and clung to them with such desperation that he could not move them. . . . [H]e cried in utter stupefaction: "What sort of little monster is this?" . . . (JR, 4)

This incident, said Judith, "clearly explained the opinion I was later to have of life." She was always headstrong, and, at the moment of her baptism, when the ritual salt was placed on her tongue, she first commented on its quality, as she says in her memoirs, and then said that she would like a bit more.

At a very young age, Judith was sent away to be nursed and raised, since nothing was to interfere with Gautier's career and necessary earnings. Having also another child, Toto, to support by another mistress, Eugénie Fort, he was in a doubly vulnerable and needy position. Judith hated the convent to which she was sent, Notre-Dame-de-la-Miséricorde, and tried first to starve herself, and then to take poison. Finally she was released and taken home, where her affection was concentrated on her nurse, Damon. When, at the end of Judith's life, she was the constant companion and, presumably, lover of a much younger woman, Suzanne Meyer-Zundel, born in 1882 (and renowned mostly for her ability to make flowers out of bread-crumbs). Her love life seemed to make a perfect circle, with a reversal of ages: young, she loved an older woman; older, she loved a younger woman.

Judith already a skilled writer when very young, was encouraged by her father to write art criticism. Widely read, deeply learned, and skilled in many areas, she was also of a staggering beauty, like a Greek statue, said her admirers. She posed for painters—most notably John Singer Sargent—and was the inspiration for and most probably the mistress of Victor Hugo, as well as the muse of Wagner's *Parsifal*, which she translated into French, and whose characters she rendered as wooden puppets, to perform the opera in miniature for her friends. Her adoration of the Master was intense, and inspired one of her autobiographical volumes in *Le Collier des jours*, the volume called *Auprès de Wagner (Wagner at Home.)*

All of this and more. She became versed in Chinese very early, through Tin-Tun-Ling, a friend of her father's known for being very light-fingered and not devoid of arrogance. Hired as an assistant to Stanislas Julien, the titular professor of Chinese at the Collège de France, he had, during an argument, declared that Professor Julien knew not one word of Chinese. He was of course dismissed from his position. When he had suggested to Judith that he might teach her the language, she replied by turning several somersaults, always the enthusiast.

She had been smitten by the Orient upon seeing two Japanese in native dress once, on a shopping expedition in the London Arcade, and really never returned from that faraway land. "I am Chinese," she said, "the reincarnation of an ancient Chinese princess." Théophile Gautier not only arranged for her to bring home precious Chinese manuscripts from the Bibliothèque Nationale in its early incarnation as the Bibliothèque Impériale (he had said how useful they would be in her studies, and who could refuse Théophile Gautier?), but used her as his willing assistant. For *Le Roman de la Momie*, she, at age eleven, handed him the pictures—becoming smitten by the spell of Egypt—and for *Spirite*, she furnished details of her life in that horrendous convent to which she had been sent when small. He helped her get her early art and music criticism published, criticism that often had his tone, and was widely admired—as were all her writings, from early to mature.

She was gifted with not just an "indefinable wildness" and brilliance, but the capability of adoration. Catulle Mendès, a great friend of the symbolist poet Stéphane Mallarmé, she adored, longed to marry, married, and was betrayed by—he had had, already before their marriage, a composer mistress for several years, the beautiful golden-haired Augusta Holmès, mother of his five children—and he never fully reciprocated Judith's love. As for Augusta, adding the accent grave to her name, which had been just plain Holmes before the transformation by the accent, made her feel more French. Very chic. She was César Franck's favorite pupil, and held her own court, in her father's place at Versailles, of composers and artists, with Villiers de l'Isle-Adam, Gounod, Saint-Saëns, and the painter Georges Clairin, who thought her "more a goddess than a woman." (JR, 35) Saint-Saëns said "we are all of us in love with her" and wanted to marry her.

Judith's father was infuriated by the matrimonial designs upon his beloved daughter of the handsome blond and much-adored Catulle—whose angelic appearance belied his cruel, sadistic and deceitful nature, and whose treacherous reputation, not his Jewish ancestry, put Théophile off. He left Ernesta in rage when she sided with Catulle against him and facilitated the wedding, for which Gustave Flaubert, who had always been an object of admiration for and close friend to Judith, acted as one of her witnesses, while Villiers de l'Isle-Adam and Leconte de Lisle acted as Catulle's witnesses. But many found it a sad affair, as it proved to be.

As Judith's biographer, Joanna Richardson, put it, "Judith loved Catulle with all the theatrical passion of the Grisis. . . . She loved him with all the Romantic love that Théophile Gautier could express. She loved him with all the fervour of youth, and of first love." (JR, 33) And she quotes Judith, who wanted to shout out Catulle's name, who found it impossible to talk of anything else, whose headstrong imagination ran delightfully wild with her love, wanting to rush into his lodgings to "ask the nooks and crannies and the drawers if it is true that you love me. They must know, but they are also your accomplices, they wouldn't tell me the truth." (JR, 34)

During their marriage, Mendès was often impoverished. "Why oh why don't poets like me have sufficient pensions so we can write our sonnets and still feed our wives?" Thus he complained to Mallarmé, and at one point suggested that the two couples live together, sure that their wives would get along. Nothing would have been less sure, and the communal living did not occur. But the couple saw a great deal of the other Parnassians, who met in the modest fifth-floor apartment of Leconte de Lisle at 8, boulevard des Invalides every Saturday. (It was a great time for weekly salons: Théophile Gautier held his on Thursdays, at which he served sausages, salami, olives, and cold fish with Judith's mayonnaise, and the Mendès held theirs on Sundays. Some scrimping the rest of the week meant one could serve one's friends something worthwhile.) Leconte de Lisle, ponderous and immense, who frowned to keep his monocle on, "had all our admiration and affection," said Mendès, faithfully attending, with Judith, de Lisle's court, where the group included Théodore de Banville, Stéphane Mallarmé, and Paul Verlaine before his decline.

The Mendès couple, soon to disintegrate, had no children together, and Judith was never to give birth. There is some speculation that Cosima Wagner's excessive reluctance to discuss with Judith small babies, like her own beloved Siegfried—alleging Judith's purported dislike of tiny ones—may have had to do with Judith's infertility. But who knows? The Mendès' dwelling at 50, rue des Martyrs, was well named for what Judith suffered over her husband's lack of affection. In some of her affections, she was more rewarded: Victor Hugo she adored, and he adored her, thereby greatly wounding the famously longsuffering Juliette Drouet, his mistress for almost forty years, who was sixty-six when Hugo, seventy, began his affair with Judith, and who had had to put up with many such affairs, none quite so intense on both sides as this one.

That last affair, between Hugo and Judith, beginning in 1872, and enduring—but of which there is no certain proof—had helped Judith separate from Catulle Mendès, which she did in 1874, a separation made official in 1878. Hugo was never one to be remarkably subtle about his love affairs. In his diary of March 4, 1872, he recorded that he "went home with Mme Judith, O, to look for some obscure poems . . ." The O stood, it seems, for his first impassioned kiss with her (*oscula*). Subsequently, he began to call on her at 4, Cité Trévise, where she now lived, wrapped in her Japanese kimonos, her face painted white and her eyes circled black with kohl. When asked once why she wore such a thick layer of makeup, she replied that under that mask, her husband—who was in any case used to seeing actresses with many layers of paint—would never see her growing old.

When her father was dying, on July 12, 1872, Hugo, always an admirer of Gautier father and daughter, wrote a sonnet, *Ave, Dea*, a tribute to his latest mistress, based on the similarities between beauty and death. It has to be said that Hugo's sonnets for Judith have all the clichés of High Romanticism:

> La mort et la beauté sont deux choses profondes
> Qui contiennent tant d'ombre et d'azur qu'on dirait
> Deux soeurs également terribles et fécondes
> Ayant le même énigme et le même secret;
>
> O femmes, voix, regards, cheveux noirs, tresses blondes,
> Brillez, je meurs! ayez l'éclat, l'amour, l'attrait,
> O perles que la mer mêle à ses grandes ondes,
> O lumineux oiseaux de la sombre forêt!
>
> Judith, nos deux destins sont plus près l'un de l'autre
> Qu'on ne croirait, à voir mon visage et le vôtre;
> Tout le divin abîme apparaît dans vos yeux,
>
> Et moi, je sens le gouffre étoilé dans mon âme;
> Nous sommes tous les deux voisins du ciel, madame,
> Puisque vous êtes belle et puisque je suis vieux. (JR, 98)
>
> Both death and beauty are deep,
> So full of shade and azure they seem
> Two sisters equally terrible and fecund
> Sharing the same riddle, the same secret;
>
> Ladies! your voice, your gaze, hair black or blonde
> Shine! I am dying! flash with love, charm,
> Oh pearls the sea mingles with great waves,
> Oh bright birds of the dark forest!
>
> > Judith, our two fates are closer
> > Than one might think, seeing my face and yours;
> > The divine abyss shows in your eyes,
> >
> > And I feel the starry gulf in my soul
> > We are both near the sky, madame,
> > For you are beautiful and I am old.

Poor Juliette, re-reading the sonnet wrote to Hugo, her god: "Ave, Deo, your very humble worshipper blesses you even in your infidelities." (JR, 104) He wrote other gooey poems, such as the over-the-top one on April 4, 1874, about Judith's naked feet so winglike, her transparent radiance and pure forehead so dazzling through any darkness:

Ame, statue, esprit, Vénus,
    Belle des belles,

Celui qui verrait vos pieds nus
    Verrait des ailes.

A travers vos traits radieux
    Luit l'espérance;
Déesse, vous avez des dieux
    La transparence.
Comme eux, vous avez le front pur,

La blancheur fière,
Et dans le fond de votre azur
    Une lumière.

Pas un de nous, fils de la nuit,
    Qui ne vous sente
Dans l'ombre où tout s'évanouit,
    Eblouissante!

Vous rayonnez sous la beauté;
    C'est votre voile.
Vous êtes un marbre, habité
    Par une étoile. (JR, 107)

Soul, statue, spirit, Venus,
    Lovely of lovelies,
Gazing at your bare feet
    One gazes at wings.

Through your radiant features
    Hope shines;
Goddess, you are transparent
    As gods.

Like theirs, your forehead is pure,
    Its whiteness proud,
And in the depths of your azure
    A light.

Not one of us, sons of the night,
Who doesn't feel you
Dazzling
In the shadow where all else fades.

You radiate under your beauty
That is your veil.
In your marble
Lives a star.

Hugo died at eighty-three in 1885, on May 22 (which would have been Wagner's birthday—he died in 1883). He had, it appears, had from Judith what Wagner evidently desired. Wagner, her elder by thirty years, she adored, and he adored her—but Cosima had nothing to fear along Juliette's lines, for Wagner's passion for the Parisian who thought herself Chinese was never consummated—so the mutual passion endured. It was Judith who procured for the Master his perfumes and silks and brocades, with which he had to surround himself to prepare properly for the composition of *Parsifal*. It does not seem to enter into her memories of Wagner that he had to or chose to wear silk or satin underwear, unable to stand anything coarser against his bare skin. In any case, such a sybaritic surrounding for such a religious piece of music may seem odd to us, but Wagner told Cosima that unlike the *Ring* music, *Parsifal*, for all its celebration of religious renunciation, was supposed to have a silken shimmer, "like cloud-layers that keep separating and combining again." (Montsalvat) As for Judith's errands for the Master, nothing about her life and loves is more surprising than anything else. Despite her restraint in the matter of certain of Wagner's desires, there was a definite secrecy to her exchanges with the Master. All her correspondence with him was sent, once his operas were being performed at Bayreuth, to the barber Schnappauf there.

Judith was born, she said, a Wagnerite. Pondering her attraction to him, shared of course by multitudes, it seems to me part of her constant fascination with what was *other:* her novels, such as *Le Dragon Impérial, L'Usurpateur (The Usurper), La Conquête du paradis (The Conquest of Paradise)*, her play written with Pierre Loti, *La Fille du Ciel (The Daughter of Heaven)*, and her translation of ancient Chinese poems (*Le Livre de jade [The Book of Jade]*) and of Japanese poems (*Poèmes de la libellule [Poems of the Dragonfly]*), orientalizing in the strongest sense, are positively lush with florid description and heavy with the scent and scenes of a vision as far removed as possible from French life and sights. Judith said of herself that she was Chinese, having always been someone different from what she originally was. Her biographer, Joanna Richardson, puts it perfectly: "She had long lived in the West to which she did not belong." (JR, 176) What a strange story was hers.

Not the least fascinating part of it for us reading about her is her relation to the Master, Richard Wagner. Judith says in *Le Collier des jours (The Necklace of Days)* (which we can imagine hanging heavily about her neck) that she had no disposition for music, and disliked her music lessons intensely until one day she heard Weber's *Invitation to the Waltz*. This was clearly love at first hearing. Then she played a Bach Gavotte, and then the first book of the *Well-Tempered Clavier*. She was hooked.

Théophile defended Wagner's *Tannhauser* in an article of the *Universel Moniteur*, and in 1861 Judith, aged sixteen, attended the rehearsal, when she came to get her father at the Concerts Pasdeloup, and heard Berlioz's attack on the music, which she never forgot. She had already started her translations of Chinese poetry, and had already written a study of Baudelaire's translation of Poe's *Eureka*, which Théophile had published, to her surprise, in *Le Moniteur*. (Reading it, Baudelaire called her "the hurricane," and claimed she would eventually sink many persons. Interestingly, Judith sat for her portrait to Madame Sabatier, Baudelaire's "white muse," who frequented Théophile Gautier's Thursday salons on the rue de Longchamp.)

Judith heard, soon after reading Berlioz's attack, *The Flying Dutchman*, and was enchanted with the idea of Richard Wagner. Her husband, Mendès, whom she had married in 1866, had been no less enchanted. Writing to Wagner about *Die Meistersinger*, she was delighted to receive a very long analysis by the Master about the prelude for the third act.

Judith took the excuse of a painting exhibition in Munich she was writing up to ask to visit Wagner in Tribschen since she was going through Lucerne. She recounted at great length, in *Le Collier des jours*. her first visit to him, with the writer Villiers de l'Isle-Adam, who was as captivated by the Master as she was. Tirelessly she extolled his wonderfulness, the customs of his house, his miraculous music. The recountings fill page after page, to our own amazement. Another relatively surprising thing is that in this account, as in many subsequent ones of her visits to Wagner, and of her first visit to Victor Hugo, Catulle Mendès, who was right there with his wife, is simply eliminated from the story, whereas Villiers de l'Isle-Adam remains in it, where he belongs—but so did they both. What might have been recounted as "we" is often said as "I," as in the initial Hugo visit.

Finding Wagner at Tribschen was ideal. The landscape was just what the Master fit best into, and his dogs, Rouzemouk and Cos, were the perfect companions. (Cosima hated being called "Cos," so she called her dog that, as a guarantee that no one would dare call her by that name. Witty woman.)

His carriage took them back to their dwelling in the Hotel du Lac, while Villiers caressed the cushions of the carriage and they recounted each detail of the marvelous day. (Auprès, 40) The next day, "which rose all blue and sunlit, was delightful for us! What a fullness of joy! What a glorious future! Now we knew Richard Wagner and he knew us! Come early tomorrow, he had said, which was more and better than just politeness: the Master liked having disciples, we sensed it." The children, waiting in the salon, greeted them, as if they hadn't just met yesterday. Such excitement. The bird song of Siegfried sounded far more impressive in that "sanctuary of sanctuaries, holy of holies, the studio of Richard Wagner." (Auprès, 40–50) (We continue to notice the absence of Catulle, present in actuality, just not in his wife's recounting.) Everything Wagner told them about his life and its events, all the indignities he had suffered, from maximal to minimal, produced on the visitors "an intense magnetising impression. We passed through all the states he described: enthusiasm, indignation, despair." If, however, the listeners were too upset by such tales, he would make a joke of it all. Even his attentiveness to his dog Russ came under discussion by the adepts of the Master, because such an affectionate preoccupation "revealed in this prodigious being . . . an infinite goodness, a limitless altruism." (Auprès, 50)

And on and on. When, however, Judith took it upon herself to write for the public about his home life, "Wagner at Home," he hated it. This was his mystery, and he had to keep it that way. She repented, of course, but continued her voluminous recounting in the pages we now read in *Le Collier des jours*. (C, 62) What is a bit strange about these recollections is their lack of humor, their downright idolizing worshipfulness. But of course, Judith was indeed gifted for admiration, finding Victor Hugo incomparably attractive and Franz Liszt incomparably noble. And, when Liszt wanted to find out her opinion about his daughter Cosima's leaving her husband, the composer Mahler, for Wagner, she was of course (given Wagner's superhuman wondrousness) completely on Cosima's side. To Liszt's relief, she concurred with his own judgment of the matter. "When it's a matter of a being so above humankind as Richard Wagner, the prejudices and even the laws of men have no more value. Who couldn't submit with joy to the fascination and the prestige of genius?" Absolutely, said Judith to Liszt, and you would have done the same thing, in Cosima's place. No obstacle, said Judith, should be placed in the way of "the magnificent outcome she has the right to expect." Ah, said the father, I am in complete agreement and actually wanted to ask you to tell her. Relief on all sides.

Ah, the joy of life with the Wagners. The Master rose at six, had his bath, returned to bed and read until 10, then worked from 11 to 2, at which time there was the main dinner, then a drive, and he would work until supper at 8, a repast instituted for his guests, and subsequently kept as a delightful custom. There would be cold meats, salads, pastries, and fruits, accompanied by champagne Chandon (for Chandon was one of Wagner's admirers, and gave him more than he could consume).

All sorts of events now transpired. *Das Rheingold* was to be put on in Munich, and the king was to come, but the set by an untalented Perfall seemed unspeakably terrible. Wagner refused to let the show go on unless there was a rehearsal, and Perfall was threatening to dismiss the conductor, Hans Richter. Wagner lamented:

> You remember this sentence from *King Lear*: It's not yet the worst when you say to yourself "It's the worst." Not only do they refuse me the single rehearsal I wanted and dismiss Richter for not being obedient to Perfall, but they are sending me away from Munich again. It seems I am a public danger, and my life is threatened. (Auprès, 184)

Richter was always present: once Wagner was eager to have the guests hear *Die Meistersinger*, particularly difficult to play on the piano, and Wagner was not a very good pianist. Richter rushed to the piano to play a chord right above the Master's fingers. Oh, the wonderful family scenes, with heavy little "Fidi," or Siegfried, stretching of his arms to show how tall he is, sitting in Judith's lap to enjoy his usual biscuits dipped in Madeira. (168) And the Master himself: "I will always see him, under his large grey felt hat, his luminous blue eyes, his laughing mouth, so delicately drawn above the prominent chin, with this scarf of yellow satin crossed over his breast because of the morning coolness." (Auprès, 188)

The same year that the Franco-Prussian war was declared, Wagner wrote Judith, now back in Paris, about her godson Siegfried's baptism. She attended the opening of the Bayreuth theatre in 1876, joined Wagner in his box, saw him frequently, and his passion increased. He wrote in anguish: "Could it have been for the last time that I held you in my arms this morning? No! I shall see you again—I want to see you! Because I love you! Adieu—Be good to me!" (Monsalvat) Judith was responsive, if not to his passion, then to him as her religion: that much is in no doubt.

In September of 1881, she returned to Bayreuth, to Wahnfried, the Master's house, to marvel again at his habits and his genius. After his morning work, he would sound the bell for his guests and show them his page of *Parsifal* on his work table. (Auprès, 234) It was declared by Liszt and of course Judith to be "a new miracle." Wagner wanted to believe that the meaning of the name was "a mad Persian fellow," wrongly deriving the title from Persian. Never mind the etymological truth. "The old troubadours just didn't understand Arabic, said the Master. "Parsifal means Parsi (think of the Persians and their adoration of fire), and Fal means mad, but in an elevated sense, that is, an unlearned man, but with genius. The English word 'fellow' seems to be related to this oriental root. You will soon learn why this naive man bore this Arabic name." (Auprès, 245) But of course Judith knew that the name was originally Parsival, or Perce-Vallée, meaning a man who fears nothing, passes through everything. Said Wagner: "I don't care about the meaning of Arabic words, and I hope that in my public to come there won't be too many orientalists." So Parsifal remained the mad Parsi, and cut his brilliant swath under that name, triumphant in 1882. (Auprès, 245-6) For the première, Judith sat with Wagner in his box, as he wept, declaring that he would have to have been twenty to enjoy it. And on Judith's last visit to him, as she recounted it, he murmured "Life is a tragedy."

On his side, Wagner was naturally intrigued by Judith's beauty and worshipful adoration of himself and his music, and continually wrote her impassioned letters. "Dear soul, sweet friend! I love you still! . . . Oh how I should love to embrace you again, dear sweet one! . . . I pity you your life. But everything is to be pitied. And I above all should be pitied if I followed your advice to forget you." (JR, 125) Judith bought clothes for Cosima, as she did for Richard, and remained devoted to both of them. It seems likely that she and the Master had no carnal relation of the sort Judith had with Victor Hugo, who was more physically attractive to her. As for the relation between the two masters, each loathed the thought of the other's receiving the admiration due to himself alone.

The German Master was particular, especially when he was composing rare works like *Parsifal*, his masterpiece. On November 22, 1877, he wrote Judith:

> I want to have the rarest and most beautiful covering for my chaise longue—a covering which I shall call Judith! Listen! Find me one of those silk materials which they call "lampas," or something like that. A yellow satin background—as pale as possible—sprinkled with networks of flowers—roses; not too big a pattern, because it isn't for curtains; it's generally used for small pieces of furniture. If there isn't any yellow, then very bright *blue*. I will need six meters.

> All of this for the good mornings *of Parsifal!*
> Goodbye, my dearest, my *dolcissima anima.* Your RW (JR, 129)

Imagine Judith's joy at having a sofa covering named after her! But then, none of this is easy to imagine.

Then, the next month, he worries more — chests she has sent have not arrived, and concerns abound, as is evident in a letter of December 18, 1877:

> Cancel the pink satin entirely: there would be too much of it, and it would be good for nothing. Can I expect the two remnants that I mentioned in my *last* letter? The brocade can be reserved: I'm inclined to order 30 metres, but perhaps the colours can be changed to suit my taste even more: in other words, the fawn-striped material would be silver-grey, and the blue *my* pink, very pale and delicate. . . . For the rest do not think ill of me! I am old enough to indulge in childish pursuits! I have three years of *Parsifal* ahead of me, and nothing must tear me away from the peaceful tranquility of creative seclusion. . . . .

It seemed never-ending, his requests and her setting about trying to accomodate them. He wrote on February 6, 1878, to ask for more rose water, for he had broken a little bottle of it, and some rose-powders, and, above all, please would she:

> be so kind as to let me know *immediately* and in a word if you have found the lilac satin (Ophelia!) since my decision to buy it depends upon your answer. Dearly beloved! I have finished the 1 st act; you shall have a sample of it. . . . Cosima continues as ever before filled with feelings of admiration and gratitude towards you on account of the Japanese dress and all the other things you have chosen for her.

But Cosima never, according to Judith's December diary, really thought that *Parsifal* could be translated into French. Then she found Richard burning some of the correspondence with Judith, about *Parsifal* and the errands associated with it. So quite, inevitably, those errands ended for Judith, and began for the devoted Cosima. And, furthermore, he asked Judith, in a letter of February 15, 1878, "Be considerate towards Cosima: write to her properly and at length. I shall be told everything. Do not stop loving me!"

Apparently, she did not. When, many years later, her companion Suzanne Meyer-Zundel inquired of her about Wagner's love for her, Judith explained that all had not been flowers and perfume in the

pattern of the relation. Not only was his desire for her not reciprocated—she preferred Hugo's person—but Judith herself had probably always been more practical than the Master, and, most certainly,
less arrogant about her being. All the same: "Oh, sighed Judith, that
love was as heavy as a paving-stone; it was always weighed down by
the sad reflection: 'Too late'—by that atrocious thing, Regret. For he
really felt that it was I who should have been his wife, his true other
half, 'his female,' as he said." (JR, 169) And Wagner had once asked if
she would have liked a son by him. To which she replied that she
would have liked to, but reminded him that he had, after all,
Siegfried. No need of another. Alas.

Like Mathilde Wesendonck before her—the inspiration for *Tristan
und Isolde*—Judith felt the pressure of Richard Wagner's feelings and
felt particularly connected to *Parsifal*. He sent her the Good Friday
Spell from the opera, which she translated first into literal French,
then into a language adapted to the music. But she was not going to
succumb to his advances, for which Cosima could be grateful. And for
much else since, Judith was a good friend to her, as to Wagner. They
had made her the godmother to Siegfried, for whom she perfected
her marionettes representing Wagnerian figures. She had been fascinated by little articulated wooden dolls as a child, and, as with so
many elements of her childhood—her assisting her father with his
exotic tales, her overwhelming love for her nurse, her fascination
with things and manuscripts Chinese—these elements continued to
mark her life.

Judith loved writing about the Master: in 1882, she had published a work on *Richard Wagner et son oeuvre poétique*, before writing
the remembrances of his home in 1903 and 1909, *Le Troisième
Rang du Collier*, translated as *Wagner at Home*. It may well be that
writing about her adored composer gave her some slight comfort
in a time in which she felt unwell, lonely, and "wretchedly uncertain of her future." (JR, 178) In any case, all three volumes of her
autobiography *Le Collier des jours: Souvenirs de ma vie* are full of wit,
humor, and pessimism. At the opening, Judith recounts her birth,
which took place in the absence of her father, away in Africa. When
she was two weeks old, he met her wearing an African burnouse
and with a small lioness upon his knee. The family was nothing if
not colorful.

About the first volumes of *Le Collier*, of 1902 and 1903, Remy de
Gourmont, not always the most enthusiastic of reviewers, delivered a
rave notice, about her writing and her self: "Judith Gautier knows

every language, living or dead, she knows every literature, philosophy and religion, and, when she writes, it is with the smiling innocence of a surprised and enchanted young girl." (JR, 178)

As for the last volume and her relation to her composer, for her entire life, she was a defender of Wagner. And he, looking over at her, found she had the eyes of someone who had just contemplated the divinity. Indeed, they had, for her, and also for him. She and Villiers, like Théophile, felt part of the company of the elect, ready to champion the Master against allcomers.

> Obviously there is born, when a new genius is revealed, a little group who can understand him, can form around him, this devoted batallion which has to defend him, console him for the universal hatred, sustain him in his Golgotha, affirming his divinity. My vocation was without any doubt that of a disciple of this new God, to understand and believe in him, for no one had influenced me. My faith had no need of a conversion on the road to Damascus. (Auprès, 247)

So that was her religion. Her belief in the German was balanced, on the other side, by her respect for and attraction to Victor Hugo, the exiled Frenchman.

Judith Gautier was a striking beauty when young and was always an independent thinker, caring little for society's norms: she dressed unlike others, thought unlike others, wrote unlike others. John Singer Sargent's superb painting of her, *A Gust of Wind* in the Detroit Institute of the Arts, shows her standing on the St.-Enogat dunes, in a long white silk or satin frock and matching hat, which she has to hold on with her left hand against the wind blowing vigorously, as she sweeps up her long hem with her right hand, stepping through some tall grasses on a cliff, with a large swish of blue sky and gauzy white clouds behind her. Her step and her figure seen from below, seem free and elegant the portrait is altogether admiring.

Rumors floated about when, in the summer of 1883, Sargent was staying with the Gautreaus at Les Chênes in Paramé, near St. Enogat, painting the famous portrait of Madame Gautreau as *Madame X*, with the falling black spaghetti strap over her shoulder, now gracing the Metropolitan Museum. Were they involved? From all we know of Sargent, more than a platonic friendship seems unlikely. He seems to have been more attracted to Henry James and other men than to women. It was Judith's beauty he drew, and that drew him. A full-length portrait of her leaning on the piano against a dark background pictures her in a full-sleeved kimono, a bow at the base of the V neck, a flower in her piled-up hair. Her eyes gaze into the distance from a face with a pensive expression. She was always described as mentally superactive, but as physically impassive, like a Greek or Oriental statue. But this exterior contained an inner violence, the equal of her early passion.

Judith Gautier was rarely inactive, from the time at which, at the age of seventeen, she translated her oriental poems (*Le Livre de jade*, as Judith Walter), and wrote her oriental tales, such as *Le Dragon Impérial*, written at twenty-two as Judith Mendès, then *L'Usurpateur*, under the same name., Then, in 1887, under the name Judith Gautier, she wrote *La Conquête du paradis*, changing names on her entrance to paradise, like any self-respecting Franco-Chinese woman of Romantic temperament and creative impulse. Subsequently, in 1913, she herself wrote the *Lettres inédites de Madame de Sévigné*, under the pretext of simply finding and editing them. Her Oriental plays and novels are endlessly romantic, decorative, splendid in scenery and imagination, convincing in detail. They begin and end with major, splashy scenes.

However, when she was still the very young Judith Walter, her translations of Chinese poems in *Le Livre de jade (The Book of Jade)* in 1867 were far quieter and less showy. As she points out in the prelude to the poems, the glory of poets in China resides precisely in the slow reception and long lasting respect for the single poem. Poets meeting might share the verses they had composed, and, on some extraordinary occasions, someone might ask to copy one, on a tablet; then it might be sung, or even recopied. Often they were written on a door, with no writer's name attached. People would stop, discuss or interpret the poem, and perhaps, as the supreme compliment, copy it again.

In the eighth century, Judith pointed out, a group of individual poems like scattered leaves, on delicate paper or white satin, might be gathered like a bouquet; but never in the lifetime of the poet. They might be sung to the accompaniment of the Chinese lyre, the *Kine*, after the lighting of perfumes: "the sacred Kine, which was to vibrate only before those who were worthy to hear it." For the very chords of the Kine "would break if they were heard by an impious ear. . . . 12 centuries before Orpheus, 15 before David, and before Homer—the Chinese poets sung their verses." (*Book of Jade*, 10)

But then, in Judith's writing, the splash took over. Her novels and plays read as high drama in the romantic mode, with Wagnerian elements set in the Oriental fashion. There is a lot of dying in dignity and high style, accompanied by the fanfare of chosen fate, the plots both deeply Oriental and calling on all possible associations of courage and suicide, nobility and sacrifice. The appeal of her writing lies in its exoticism of spectacle and psychology. As Judith Mendès, now married, more and more unhappily, to Catulle Mendès, whom she greatly loved and had been terribly hurt by, she made a marriage of creation and imagination with Chinese history and legend, preferable to her real one.

A few examples will suffice to give the tone, which is well-nigh untranslatable, given its Franco-Chinese garments. One of her best novels, the ultra-colorful *Dragon Impérial*, written when she was twenty-two, was serialized in 1868 in *La Liberté*, and greatly admired by Edmond de Goncourt, Villiers, Anatole France, and Mallarmé. The strong opening shows a laborer, Ta-Kiang, hammering against and chopping into the harsh terrain he is working: his rebellious nature is instantly perceived, and the reader knows he is no ordinary laborer. Indeed not. A poet, Ko-Li-Tsin, who is watching him, in surprise at the presumed peasant's anger against the earth, longs to write the best poem in the land, for that way, he will be able to marry the daughter of the mandarin governor, though he has never seen her. His passive attitude is the opposite of that of the laboring peasant: tall and haughty, bearing himself like a cedar tree, while his forehead resembles the sinister moon in a raging sky. The poet's eyes blink, and move about according to his joyous or strange thoughts, "which made you think, by their flashing, of the sun glancing on the water. His light clothes were vivacious and sparkling like this delicate being." (*Le Dragon Impérial*)

> The poet spoke in verse, but suddenly perceived Ta Kiang's shadow, like the huge reflection of a winged dragon, and said to himself: "If the shadow of a man takes the form of a dragon which humbly follows the steps of his master, this man will hold one day in his hand the handle of the imperial jade sceptre."

And one day, Ta-Kiang does indeed become emperor, accepts nothing from men, and kills himself. The poet cries: "The Emperor of China is dead! A glorious death! On the battle field! And the Dragon is carrying him on high!" (D, 300) Alas, Yo-Men-Li, the girl who loved him, will die with him, as the prophetic image had warned, a tide of blood, regular like the ebb and flow of a sea, had wet her feet and her dress. So she dies, and her severed head continues to watch the scene: "It was there, so white, with the great sad eyes, turned to the side where the old men had taken away the head of Ta –Kiang."

"Ah," cries the poet to the executioner, "hurry up and take me, I am bored all alone." But just then, in a carriage behind silk curtains, appears the governor's daughter, blushing in the shadow of the drapes, and calling to him. "Ah," he cries again, "You come to give me a supreme joy and render my death glorious?" "Oh no," she says, "don't speak of dying; I am bringing you life . . ." (D, 309) But he had to die, because his friends had already left: "I have to rush to rejoin them."

> "That's the way you love me!" Tsi-Tsi-Ka cried!
> Yes, said Ko-Li-Tsin, "I love you enough not to give you a cowardly and dishonored spouse. I die so you can be a glorious widow."—but still I have to write the poem with which I won you.
> And he wrote that poem in the blood of his companions on the white facade of a house nearby. (D, 310)

The poem says: "your memory is engraved in our spirit, as in times past there were engraved the noble deeds of the three sovereigns on the shell of the Divine Tortoise!" . . .

> And soon the executioner showed everyone the poet's head. It was smiling.
> The evening came . . . a great cloud had the form of a winged animal of smoke, blood, and gold. It was the sunset of the Dragon. (D, 310)

Some of the same elements of glorious death, of noble sacrifice, and omens marvelous and terrible, are found in all of Judith Mendès/Gautier's writings. They are instantly recognizable by their tone and spectacular detail—as she was herself, always dressed in Oriental costumes, with her impassive face noble above its clothing, with an Oriental languor: like a "Goddess of Nonchalance," said a visitor. (JR,20) Her writings do not feel simply Orientalizing: they feel authentic in their strangeness. The impassive and noble elements make a strange contrast with Judith's tormented life during her years of passion and impassioning of others.

An epilogue to Judith Gautier's novel *La Conquête du Paradis* (*The Conquest of Paradise*) of 1877, points out how the dream of India in the nineteenth century was so prevalent, with its ideal of an exotic and fabulous imperial utopia. All colonialization can be read as the "murder of what makes the Other different." Judith Gautier is dreaming of an India now lost to us. The novel begins on a starry night: "But it is an

Indian night streaming with stars. The sea, all foaming with sparks, seems to be rolling embers about, mingling ribbons of fire." And it ends in similar spectacular manner, with a "flight of swans, whose snowy feathers took fire in the sunlight and seemed to hover above the lovers, like a premonition of glory and happiness."

Nature and its omens and premonitions are always in accord with Gautier's chosen figures. Nothing is detachable from anything else, in the sky, sea, or human heart.

Her play *La Fille du Ciel* was written with her close friend Pierre Loti, whom she had met during a costume ball. She had been dressed as Cleopatra and he as Pharaoh. She had complimented him on his possessing an extraordinary thing, like a detail found on Greek statues: on his sandaled feet it was clear that his second toe was longer than the big one. After that, they struck up a correspondence entirely in Egyptian hieroglyphs, as was only fitting. The play had originally been intended for the great Sarah Bernhardt, who had longed, as she had said to Loti, to star in a Chinese play. When Loti replied that he might work with Judith on such a play, Sarah had replied "I adore that exquisite woman." (JR, 179) However, the divine Sarah became impatient over the time it took to write it, and then heartily detested the four monologues in the second act. (But, said Judith, she always has monologues.) In any case, although the play was never produced, it was finally published in 1911, and translated as *The Daughter of Heaven*. This quite remarkable and ultimately Romantic drama has as its topic the terrible wound of the Chinese nation lamenting being conquered by the Manchus of Tartary. It is explained in the preface that "the Chinese nation never ceased to mourn the ancient dynasty nor to hope for its restoration."

When the Tartar Emperor in Peking was about to triumph over the old dynasty in NangKing, the emperor Tai-Ping-Tien-Ko, who had reigned for seventeen years, decreed there be no surrender of the conquered. Rather, the vanquished set fire to their own palace and burned themselves alive, while the women hung or strangled themselves, or plunged into the lakes. The Emperor, in his shroud of yellow silk embroidered with dragons, poisoned himself. This history, once suppressed, was thereby restored to life by Judith and her friend. The words exchanged are full of a kind of flowery ancient-speak, dignified and lofty; I translate them here roughly from the French, at sufficient length to give an idea of the play. It scarcely lends itself to staging.

The Tartar Emperor, clearly in love with the Chinese Empress, addresses her: Daughter of Heaven, deign to raise your eyes to gaze

upon the heart-broken conqueror who bows before you. Deign to look
and to recognize him. . . . But can you feel anything save utter hatred
for him?

Empress (*Far away, her eyes still lowered.*)
To recognise him, I do not need to hear his voice again nor to gaze
upon his face. . . . Before I was brought in here, I knew full well into
whose presence I was coming. (H, 138)

. . .

Emperor
Your voice is no longer yours. Your eyes are no longer yours. You stand
here before me, yet your soul seems to be at an infinite distance. I did
not expect to find you so, and you frighten me. The Majesty of death is
upon you.

Empress
They are calling to me from the Land of the Shades. Allow me to cross
the threshold soon, from you I can accept no mercy. My faithful ones,
my warriors are wondering at my delay in rejoining them, and my son
is listening to catch the echo of my footfall behind him on the dark
path. (H, 172)

Her attendants are dead all around her, and she wants the poison held
by the Emperor. She desires, she says, only to sleep near her son,
whose porcelain tomb will be enveloped by two long rows of dark
cedars. "Will you grant me the favour to sleep near him?" she asks
(H, 173) When she draws the dagger from the folds of her robe, the
Emperor takes it from her, promising her instead a poison, more dignified: "Lustrous pearls under a thin leaf of gold. One passes into space
in a sudden sleep, an exquisite intoxication. . . ."

He longs to save her son, and has issued a pardon, "so that at least
you may not hate me."

Empress
(*Still calm and impersonal*)
I have no hate for you.

Emperor
Of my love I have not even dared to speak to you.

Empress
I am grateful to you that you have kept our interview above that level.

Emperor
I beg of you, Daughter of Heaven, to live!

Empress (*Severely*)

But your promise, sire, your imperial word of honour. Give it to me. (*The Emperor, after another silence, kneels before her, takes the golden box from his girdle and hands it to her slowly, his face turned downward to the ground.*)

Empress (*she puts the pearls in her mouth, then throws the box to the ground, and rises in exaltation. Triumphant and dominating the room, she addresses the invisible spirits of her forefathers.*) Oh, my ancestors, behold me! Am I not glorious? You see me in that place whence you of old dominated the world, and it is upon your throne, usurped by the Tartar, that I am about to die! Your daughter has remained worthy of her race. . . . (*She seats herself on the throne again. He seats himself on the throne near her . . .*)

Empress

For I loved you. (*The Emperor arises*) And, living, I have no more the right to happiness, because it was I who lit that great funeral pyre of men's lives in my palace.

Emperor (*Interrupting, exultantly*)

O my sovereign! O my beautiful, fading flower! To hear that from your lips at the moment when they are about to grow cold forever! Oh!

Empress (*Wandering, half drawing herself away*)

Ah! Yes—I hear the great bell sounding. It is the signal, then? I am sinking—Hold me up, my beloved. Keep me from sinking thus—into the abyss. (*During an instant of silence, they remain embraced. Then the Emperor rouses himself, cries aloud in his grief, and the dead body falls back on the throne.*) (*H, 180–191*)

Final Scene

Emperor

On your knees, all of you, before the Daughter of Heaven!—
(*He kneels on the steps himself. The marble chimes are sounded. The brilliantly dressed crowd fills the throne-room, prostrating themselves before the dead.*)(*H, 183–190*)

Judith Gautier wrote many other tales of China and of Japan, which might have been labeled: "histoires merveilleuses"—as unusual as they are peculiar. They give, as one of her last titles reads, "the perfume of the pagoda" and the sense of a learned approach to details: costumes, history, objects, rituals. This daughter of Théophile was endowed with an extraordinary energy for work: writing biographies and guide books—as with her monograph for *Les Capitales du Monde* on Tokyo where she had been only in her vivid imagination—translating from Japanese as well as Chinese, writing extensive music and art criticism, including a work on *Musiques bizarres* for the 1900 world exhibition, dealing with all kinds of music Chinese, Indo-Chinese, Japanese, Javanese, Egyptian, and Malagasian, writing a classic children's story, *Mémoires d'un Eléphant Blanc/Memories of a White Elephant*, as well as many novels and plays, even one based on her father's extraordinary tale of androgyny, *Mademoiselle de Maupin*.

As she moved between her Paris apartment at 30, rue Washington and her villa, "Le Pré aux Oiseaux" (The Bird Meadow—named after Wagner's Walther von der Vogelweide in *Die Meistersinger*) in St.-Enogat, Brittany, in which she installed herself in 1877, she moved also between the worlds of art, music, and literature. Louis Benedictus, a fat composer who had adored her for years, and of whose compositions, which Judith showed to Wagner, the Master had said, rather disobligingly: "These days, everyone composes," was totally devoted to her, sharing in her affections with Suzanne Meyer-Zundel, her Alsatian companion, thirty-seven years younger, and, we assume, her lover. "An unused mother's heart," said one observer, and her most astute biographer marveled: "The woman who had once loved Catulle Mendès with passion, who had been the mistress of Hugo, the inspiration of Wagner, the love of Mohsin-Khan, the admiration of Baudelaire, Leconte de Lisle and Sargent, the woman who had enslaved Benedictus, Baudry, Armand Silvestre and innumerable other men, had now become, in her sixties, dependent on a dull, uneducated, infatuated girl." (JR, 198). In any case, she needed that unqualified devotion, and responded to it. One or the other would hold on to her companion's dress, as they went down the street. They were interdependent, and the younger one was buried in Judith's grave in the little Breton cemetery adjoining her garden, high atop the cliff at St.Enogat, where the cat Lilith had let herself die of starvation, keeping watch over Judith's remains.

Judith had been faithful also, to her dogs, birds, and cats. She would travel back and forth from Paris in the train, reserving several extra seats for her pets, for whom and for herself she always had a "Balzac," a concoction of sardines and butter mixed. At home, during another period, the cats were Satan and Juliette. The animal population changed, but not Judith's preference of them to people in general, save the exotic Orientals, who would grace her Sunday afternoons in their elaborate costumes, when she would wear her flowing silk robes decorated with butterflies and roses. She had a particular fondness for her cats; for Lilith and Bébé, Iblis and Crevette, she would decorate a Christmas tree and make little angels and figures out of clay, some of whom would hold a Union Jack on high, thus mixing all the customs happily together. Among writers gifted at mixing customs and countries and genres and tones, Judith Gautier holds a particular place, and holds it with a truly eccentric dignity.

She was perceived as solitary, an anchorite, creating a faraway world of her own. She had once said to Suzanne that each person had an emotional core "besides which nothing else exists." Hers was her betrayed love for Catulle. Behind her she left a prose poem about the temple she had built to her faith in him, terribly betrayed:

> O you whom I adore without reserve, tremble with fear to the very marrow of your bones!
>
> For I shall trust neither God nor Satan to accomplish my revenge.
> I shall tear you from the altar which you have usurped, I shall tear your body asunder, and I shall drag you out of this life.
>
> And, through the infinite abysses, through the whole eternity of time, I shall pursue you with my cries of rage, and I shall drive you mad with the ever-increasing cruelty of my hatred, the hatred which nothing will ever assuage. (JR, 169)

Yet the hatred was inside, and the generosity and love were outside, shining even under her masked face. She had always a sense of fidelity: to her pets and friends and lovers and father. And he to her. "Judith," declared Théophile Gautier, "has much more talent than Madame Sand, and so, as you will see, she will never be successful." (JR, 23)

CHAPTER 2

SUZANNE VALADON

BEYOND MODEL AND MOTHER

Vive l'amour!

— *Suzanne Valadon, end of letter to Le Masle, July 13, 1937*

Suzanne Valadon was a model and a painter, but has been until recently thought of chiefly as the mother of Maurice Utrillo. She was also known to me as the model for many figures in one of the soupiest paintings I ever encountered, Puvis's *Le Bois sacré* (*The Sacred Wood*), the triumph of the 1884 Salon, as the model for his *Jeunes filles au bord de la mer* of 1879, and as the model for many other painters.

Known as a great male painter's model, the female painter is rarely well known as herself. A famous example is the painter Victorine Meurent, seen in Manet's *Olympia* and in his *Matador*. In this case, it turned out that Suzanne Valadon was the first woman painter ever to paint naked males and females together, and a true eccentric as well as a great artist, whose former studio at 12 rue Cortot is now the Musée de Montmartre.

But let me take it from the beginning. Born in 1865, Marie-Clémentine Valade was the daughter of a seamstress. (Later, she changed both her birth date, making herself two years younger, and her name.) She herself was first a seamstress and laundress, then a circus performer until a severe fall from a trapeze, after which she turned to modeling, between 1880 and 1883. She was the preferred model of Auguste Renoir, twenty-four years older than she, as well as of Puvis de Chavannes forty years older; and she was Toulouse-Lautrec's exhausted drinking woman, leaning disconsolate on the table: *La Buveuse* or *Gueule de bois* (*The Hangover*) of 1887–89, of his

Poudre de riz (*Young Woman at a Table*, 1887) and the star of his *Le Cirque*—appropriately, since she had been a circus performer. These were among her many lovers, and the rest of her story seems equally romanticizable. She is heroine and whore, the mother of Maurice Utrillo who was a roaring drunk and addict as well as a famous painter. Because she was so well-known as the model for elderly painters, Toulouse-Lautrec said to her one day: "You who pose for old men, you should call yourself Susanna." Indeed she did, from then on, signing her work "Suzanne Valadon" or "S. Valadon," but putting always this taken-on name in small letters, usually just as "S." This colorful creative woman was not always a partisan of the straight truth, post-dating her early drawings as well as her birth year.

Most famously, she was Renoir's voluptuous nude, represented in canvas after canvas: notably in *Les Baigneuses (The Bathers)*. Later, Suzanne told the critic Tabarant that she had posed for all three of Renoir's dance paintings: "I am the dancer who smiles as she falls into the arms of her partner, and I am also the fashionable young lady in long gloves and a dress with a train. I also sat for a scene at Bougival. As for the nudes, Renoir painted several of me." (V, 59) These paintings of the *Dance in the City*, the *Dance in the Country*, and the *Dance at Bougival* all date from 1883. But in the painting called *Dance in the Country*, another face is featured. The story goes that Aline Charigot, Renoir's blonde mistress, two years older than Suzanne, burst into his studio and rubbed out Suzanne's features, so he repainted the face as hers. What confirmed Aline's jealousy was that she found Suzanne later in his arms; so she pushed her out of the studio with a broom.

Suzanne Valadon was a habituée of the Lapin Agile, and of the Cafe de la Nouvelle-Athènes, where she mingled with the artists known as "Les Intransigeants," thus the frequent epithet applied to her: "Mistress of Montmartre." She also began painting, but after 1883 and the birth of her son Maurice, when she was eighteen, she returned to modelling out of necessity. Who was the child's father among her lovers at the time: Renoir, or Puvis de Chavannes? (The latter painter, a grand and prideful old man, was not about to claim parenthood of the baby: a statement sent at his death by his great-nephew clearly announced that "in his will there is no mention of any legacy accorded to Suzanne Valadon. It is obvious that a man of the class of Monsieur René PUVIS de CHAVANNES, if he had had the slightest idea of having been the father of MAURICE UTRILLO, would have left the so-named—given the considerable wealth that was his—an amount at least the equivalent of those he left to his family.") (Masle)

Or was the father perhaps Adrian Boissy, a singer at the Lapin Agile, or someone called Bagdad? A letter in the archives (Masle, 156) states that in 1888 or 1899, Monsieur Georges Bonne knew Suzanne Valadon in Paris: "she posed for Wertheimer, for Renoir, for Degas." Wertheimer, a very academic painter, had asked her to pose as the sailor in "The Siren's Kiss." "She was very pretty then, with regular features and strangely disturbing eyes, like a wildcat. As she posed often and we were among painters, I often saw her body which was admirable. Her skin was covered with a soft down that gave it golden reflections. You would have thought her a statue. Suzanne was an artist in her soul. . . . At my parents', Suzanne met a rich Romanian, Bagdad, who was a kind of Rothschild in his country. He was a short dark man 22 years old. Soon Suzanne who had had a child with Bagdad went off to live with him on la rue Tourlaque. At this point she was drawing on anything, even the butcher's yellow papers, in red chalk. Her mother kept Maurice for a while, and then she moved to the rue de l'Abreuvoir, after leaving Bagdad."

Well, perhaps. Or then, perhaps, the father was Miguel Utrillo, a Spanish painter in Paris? She had met him in 1883 at Le Chat Noir, founded by the Spaniard Rodolphe Salis, when Utrillo was demonstrating the "Candle dance" performed by outgoing church wardens. He was Picasso's friend in Paris and a regular at Picasso's Spanish haunt, the café-restaurant *Els Quatre Gats* in Barcelona, where he was also involved with the shadow puppet theatre based on the Parisian Chat Noir. He left Paris from 1882 to 1883, returning off and on. Suzanne destroyed his correspondence in 1934, while always admitting that he had been her first love. And she agreed, in an interview with Berthe Weil, that the son resembled Utrillo, and that, in any case, this relation made sense. (Storm, 99). A painting in the Barcelona collection of Manuel Gari de Arana, by Picasso's friend Santiago Rusiñol, shows a Paris studio in 1891, with Valadon reading quietly while Utrillo stretches out full length and fully clothed: it is in the "intimiste" style, like that of Edouard Vuillard, and feels like intimacy itself. So perhaps that latter story is the right one.

In any case, Miguel Utrillo officially acknowledged, in 1891, Maurice as his son, giving him his own name, Utrillo. As this story is usually told, Miguel asked Suzanne who the father was. "It could have been Puvis or it might have been Renoir" said Suzanne. To her alleged answer to his question about paternity, Miguel Utrillo is said to have replied, like a true gentleman: "Well, they are both fine artists, I would be honored to sign my name to the work of either of them." (V, 93–4) After his death, Miguel Utrillo's sons offered Maurice a share of their father's estate, but Suzanne signed a disclaimer. Another document Puvis had signed guaranteeing support for her and her child was torn up after his death, a fact disputed by his great-nephew.

As for her own work, Suzanne, who had always dreamed of being an artist and had sketched since she was very young, hesitated to show it, and the stories are legion about her scratching on the sidewalks of Montmartre until she was noticed by some great painter. As the mother of Maurice Utrillo, whose paintings sold far better, whose fame was far greater, whose irregular life out-irregulared hers by far, Suzanne Valadon was first destined to go down into history as a painter of horses. That stage did not last, because Suzanne moved on, as she always did.

The facts of the other side of the case are these: the painters Toulouse-Lautrec and Zandomeneghi decided that Degas had to see her drawings, and they approached him through Paul Bartholomé, closer to him than they were. Degas was astonished by the self-taught artist in her mid-twenties, of such modest background, bought a drawing she had done in red chalk of a girl getting out of the bath called *La Toilette*, and hung it in his dining room, telling her "You are one of us." She recalled later "That day I had wings." (V, 83) It was Degas, thirty years older than she, who first let her believe she could be an artist.

In 1895, Degas taught her soft-ground etching, using his own press, and they remained close friends until his death. When, in his old age and blind, he had to move, it was Valadon who found him an apartment. Calling her "terrible Maria, " he was well aware of her tempers and her uncompromising nature, and clearly admired her work and persistence. That Degas was her first patron, the first great artist to recognize her, that he was her mentor, and friend, has not received much notice, perhaps because it has not seemed a useful element in the drama of her easily romanticized story as the mistress of Montmartre.

She chose, for the rest of her life, the role of a maverick. She had many affairs, a long one with Toulouse-Lautrec, known for his sexual prowess and, shall we say, physical attributes, and a far shorter one with Erik Satie (1866–1925), who adored her. He played the piano at the Chat Noir, where in 1883 Valadon had met Miguel Utrillo, and from 1890 at the Auberge du Clou on the Avenue Trudaine. There, in the next year, he in his turn met Utrillo, who introduced him to his Catalan friends. Satie's affair with Suzanne dates from 1892 to the next year. She lived with him at 6 rue Cortot, in his attic room, for six months, from January to June 1893. At this address lived the poet Pierre Reverdy, the sometimes lover of Coco Chanel, also the painters Emile Bernard, Raoul Dufy, and Othon Friesz. Through Erik Satie, she met Debussy, Ravel, and many other musicians. (Reverdy once found the noise above him so loud that he fired his revolver at the ceiling.) Satie and Valadon spent idyllic afternoons in the Luxembourg Gardens sailing toy boats, on the afternoons when she was not with Degas.

There is a wonderful letter to Suzanne from Satie, written on March 11, 1893:

Dear little Biqui,
Impossible to stop thinking about your whole being; you are inside me completely; everywhere I see only your exquisite eyes, your gentle hands and your little child's feet.
You are happy; my poor thoughts will not wrinkle your clear forehead, neither will you worry about not seeing me at all.
For me there is only the solitude that creates emptiness inside my head and fills my heart with sadness.

Don't forget that your poor friend hopes to see you at one at least of these three rendezvous:

1. This evening at my place at eight forty-five
2. Tomorrow morning again at my place
3. Tomorrow evening at Dédé's

I should add, darling Biqui, that I shall on no account get angry if you can't come to any of these rendezvous; now I have become frightfully reasonable; in spite of the great happiness it gives me to see you.
I am beginning to understand that you can't always do what you want.
You see, little Biqui, there is a beginning to everything.
Je t'embrasse sur le coeur. Erik Satie— 6 rue Cortot (V, 101)

Her affair with Satie was a happy one, for her, and for him until she left him. After his death in 1925, in his room at Arceuil, the two portraits, by Satie of Valadon, and by her, of him, were found together.

But she had been pursued by the rich stockbroker Paul Moussis already in 1893, and finally married him at the registry office in 1896. In 1900 she taught her child Maurice to paint as therapy for alcoholism, and a few years later, met his friend André Utter, twenty years her junior. They fell in love, and then one day in 1906, Moussis, by then her husband of thirteen years, discovered her with André and pitched her out of the studio, together with her easels, paints, canvases, and drawings, and into eventual poverty again. In 1910 Moussis filed for divorce.

Suzanne's apparent promiscuity served to damn her in the eyes of the public: she had been, true enough, Puvis de Chavanne's conquest, Renoir's lover, and beloved of Toulouse-Lautrec and Erik Satie. And now she had betrayed her husband with a man far younger than herself, and been evicted from her home. Her largest painting, *Adam and Eve* of 1909, the year she met André, pictures him and herself side by side. However, André was forced to wear a giant figleaf, which she eventually made into a whole garland, in an exaggerated mode. And when she set up household with Maurice and André, her joy and relaxed moods are reflected in those of her nudes of this period. The art critic and friend of Apollinaire, André Salmon, an admirer of Valadon and of the exaggeratedly nonconformist setup, called them "the terrible trio." And, on the other hand, writers like Philippe Jullian have had an easy time portraying her as a slut such as his description of her in his book on Montmartre: "No one has ever washed her dirty linen in public so spectacularly. . . . Utrillo's martyrdom began when his mother set up house with her favorite model, André Utter. Suzanne Valadon found that the easiest thing to do was to shut her son up and make him copy postcards of Montmartre." (V, 1) Nevertheless, Valadon was making a success of herself and her career, despite all the gossip and the built-in difficulties of her adventuresome life. In 1894, she was the only woman exhibiting in the Salon de la Société Nationale des Beaux-Arts, with five drawings. In May 1898, she was exhibited in London, at the International Society of Painters, Sculptors and Engravers show in Knightsbridge, alongside Monet, her ex-lover Toulouse-Lautrec, and Degas, who was probably responsible for her inclusion, through his friendship with James Abbott McNeill Whistler.

What fascinates me is the legend as well as the life, the injustice as well as the work. Suzanne Valadon did not, like many other painters, work on her legend. Nor very successfully on her life. The others have done that for her, romanticizing her story. The most egregious romanticizer took her story and in two alternatively boring and sentimental volumes, showed "The Mistresss of Montmartre" in her fantastical life, that already needed no dramatizing: it was itself dramatic. But of course, retold, it has everything: lovers, colorful living, bouts of drinking, poverty, jealousy, near-incest, modeling and making, what have you. Like the brilliant Canadian painter Emily Carr, who ended her days living in a caravan with a great assortment of animals, some rather unusual ones, and who was and is considered both a remarkable artist and a crazed female, Valadon is the subject of widely differing points of view. Why, ask some feminist critics, is Toulouse-Lautrec's portrait of Van Gogh leaning on a table drinking called a portrait of Van Gogh, and *La Buveuse* not called a portrait of Valadon?

I feel about Valadon the exact way I feel about Carr, and the other denizens of this volume. I see in them the energy of female genius along with the courage of female eccentricity, finding that an unbeatable combination. That is the point of view I want to defend here. Valadon made her own statement of the way she painted, and wanted to paint, giving it the large title of "Nature and Painting":

> *Nature* has a total hold over me—trees, sky, water, and all beings charm me passionately, profoundly. These are the forms, the colors, the movements, which have caused me to paint, in order to try, with love and fervor, to render what I so love. In everything I have painted, not one touch, not one stroke that isn't taken from *nature. Nature* brings me to control of solid truth for the *construction* of my canvasses, conceived by me but always motivated by the emotion of life. Suzanne Valadon (Masle, 157)

As to her own version of what she wanted her story to be, there survive a few fragments scribbled down of an autobiography she was writing, called, rather grandly, *Suzanne Valadon ou l'Absolu.*

> You have to be harsh with yourself.
> the goal of my life—equilibrium—with a conscience—to look yourself directly in the face.
> This surplus—this hatred and this excess of love—you have to spill it out
> You must not put suffering in your drawing but all the same you have nothing without suffering
> All that started when I was so young, eight years old. I wrote out what I saw—I would have wished to attain, to show, so that I could keep: trees, legs—certainly I could ask that of the gods.
> I had good training in loneliness—this extreme schooling—
>
> . . .
>
> I was insulted because I told the truth
> It is the most difficult thing to be great in painting.

Art exists to make eternal this life that we detest but love its mystery . . . to transmit an act. I adore literature
Music is the most astonishing invention of man
I was haunted—my child's brain thought too much. I was a devil, I was a boy—the memory of life I peopled when I came home.
I painted at fourteen.
If you don't receive harsh blows, you have no greatness.
I was too pure.
I was so wild and prideful that I didn't want to paint—
You've no idea how much understanding a painting demands.
Others . . . saying that my mystical drawings were Michelangelos.
Always look for the why.
You have to be hard on yourself. I don't know how to ask easy things of myself. (Masle, 156)

In that document, I want particularly to emphasize the passage: "I would have wished to show . . . trees, legs—certainly I could ask that of the gods"—a most extraordinary combination to which I will return.

She further reflected on what was essential to her in painting:

I painted with what I had, not making any distinction, that is I painted truly.
It's the palette of the impressionists that enchanted me and reasoning out the answer to enduring that I always cherished. I don't mind ruining something because I could just tear it up.
. . . I tried to make for myself such a simple palette that I didn't need to think about it any more. (I made my own colors for fifteen years.)
I drew madly for when I wouldn't be able to see any more. I have eyes at the ends of my fingers.
There are some paintings I keep working on, martyr paintings.

It could also be said that she was a martyr to her son's habits and his fame. For Utrillo, increasingly successful, painted in the street, hawking his paintings to the dealers when they were barely dry, so that he could spend the money on drink. Suzanne would pay for the broken windows, glasses, bottles. With Utter, the three of them frequented the Lapin Agile, Suzanne's old haunt as a young model, still, these 30 years later, when she was 45, Degas 76, and Renoir and Toulouse-Lautrec were dead.

Now we are in 1908, hanging out with Derain, Gris, Picasso, Apollinaire, Vlaminck, Matisse. Picasso's *Demoiselles d'Avignon*—painted in the same year that Apollinaire wrote his pornographic story *Les Onze Mille Verges* — has created the furor we know about, and in the Lapin Agile, some Valadon and Utrillo paintings are on the wall. Here, a crucifixion serves as a hat-stand, and Valadon looks like some "timeless gypsy." She is described at this point, as "proud and vengeful, voluptuous and bawdy, passionate and possessive, jealous and loud-mouthed". (Gianadda, 15) Valadon's paintings are often exchanged for meals and wine for herself and André; Utrillo comes in late at night.

The scene is colorful: to Marinetti's *Futurist Manifesto* of 1909, a Lapin Agile sort of response was made in 1910 by Roland Dorgelès. He took the celebrated donkey of the Lapin Agile's beloved owner, the donkey Lolo, tied a paintbrush to her tail and several tubes of paint, one after the other. She obligingly switched her tail, and the result was entitled *Sunset over the Adriatic*. It hung in the Salon, with great success. Then *Le Matin* published the spoof manifesto signed "Joachim Raphael Boronali" (anagram of *aliboron* or jackass). It went something like this:

> Strength through excess . . . The sun is never too bright, the sky too green, the distant sea too red, the dark too black. Destroy museums, trample on their absurd exhibits, scorn carefully finished paintings, instead dazzle and yell. (V, 144)

A great success for all, especially Lolo.

In 1912, the "terrible trio" or the "profane family" as they were called, went for a long vacation and a triple attempt at painting, to the Breton isle of Ouessant. It was not a success. By this time, there were quarrels, enhanced by the bleakness of the views on and from the island. But later, in 1913, they made another try, and all went to Corsica, encountering there "a sun unlike any other, exploding, caressing, adorning and embellishing." There, Valadon painted the epic portrait of Utter as all three fishermen of Corsica, in *The Casting of the Net*. That painting was the central fascination of the 1914 Salon des Independants. And in the same year, 1914, Suzanne married Utter, who was 28; she was 49. Then he left for the front in 1914, and returned, wounded, in 1917. Suzanne, always in love with him, sped to his side.

The quite creepy Maurice Utrillo would say, to anyone who looked at the couple in the street, pointing to them: "You see that couple, I'm working for them, making their money." (V, 204) He veered between hot and cold. Of his mother, in *The Story of my Youth*, this self-described "faded rosebush" of a son wrote in a sentimental outburst dated from October 13, 1914:

> From the depths of my soul I bless and venerate my mother. I look
> upon her as a Goddess, a sublime creature full of goodness, integrity,
> charity, selflessness, intelligence, courage and devotion. She is a noble
> person, perhaps the greatest pictorial luminary of the century and of
> the world . . . alas! I failed to take her good advice and allowed myself
> to be dragged into vice by frequenting impure and lewd creatures. Alas
> and a hundred times alas! May the author of my days forgive me."
> (V, 16–17)

She would plead with him: "Cher petit Maurice, I am anxious, be
good, do not drink ever again, think of poor Utter and me." But of
course he drank again, and they continued to be seen as the "forsaken
Trio, the Trinity of the Damned." Utrillo was both a painter and a lost
cause for the moment. In 1920 he attempted suicide, and there
ensued a series of internments in hospitals and asylums. The struggle
in him between childhood and adulthood was constant, and critics
like to point out how this struggled may be reflected in Valadon's
painting of 1921: *The Cast-off Doll*.

Berthe Weill, finding Valadon overwhelming, and thinking her a
trollop at heart, would all the same have exhibitions for mother and
son, and Bernheim Jeune wrote Valadon a contract. At the shows, the
critics would like Valadon, but the public would always buy Utrillo. It
is true that Suzanne made no effort at all to please. At her openings,
she would wear unbecoming shoes, would smoke, and would leave
early, saying she had to go home and make the soup. "Never, " said
Robert Rey, who was eventually to become a curator at the Musée de
Luxembourg, "was there an artist more impolitic or more dismissive
of criticism." (V, 190) (Brava, in my view. That qualifies as eccentric
behavior of the good kind.)

In 1925, there was a show at the Pavillon de Marsan, organized by
Louis Vauxcelles, without any work of Valadon's. The women artists
included were like Marie Laurencin, twenty years younger than
Valadon, and prone to make dreamy gauzy watercolors. Marie
Laurencin was apt to make such remarks as this: "Each day I make
myself do some sewing, as it is the most feminine exercise there is: it
reminds me that I am a woman. . . . My ambition is that men should
feel a voluptuous sensation when they look at my portraits of women.
Love interests me more than painting." (V, 218) Understandably, given
this mentality, Laurencin cultivated useful friends: Colette, Gide,

Cocteau. Svelte and sophisticated in all her photographs, she was the very opposite of Valadon's chaotic life and appearance.

In the place of Laurencin's sweet-visaged females, Valadon's casually posed, powerful nudes made, on Vauxcelles and the others, just the opposite impression; so of course she was not included in this show or ones like it. André Gide described Laurencin's clothing at one of her exhibitions: "Exquisite in a sort of very open sweater, grey and artichoke green. . . ." (V, 61) Not exactly the way Valadon dressed. Vauxcelles wanted a female's work to reflect "feminine qualities: refinement and sensitivity." Not exactly what Valadon represented. Her paintings included not only the startling nudes posed in lubricious attitudes on sofas, and the agressively staring self-portraits, but also those of the "Black Venus, " one of Maurice's more noted mistresses.

Although the famed couturier Paul Poiret bought a painting in May 1917, Valadon, instead of cultivating him, rushed to the side of André Utter, wounded in 1919. Valadon's entire being and work were indeed, as she said, uncompromisingly toward the side of what she believed in, and that was not the pastel elegant woman of Laurencin. She was destined for some other form of work and life. As for Utter, his temper was, like that of Valadon and Utrillo, far from good. He repented of it frequently: in September of 1925, he writes a letter that manages to be both sincere and a bit smarmy:

> I ask forgiveness from my Suzanne, my beloved wife of whom I am so proud. I ask her forgiveness for the harm and insults and my temper which prevents her from living in tranquillity and working in peace. . . . I profoundly regret that I am so weak that I cannot control or tolerate my wife's state of nerves which is the cause of all the trouble. I only want to see her paint. . . . I love everyone who loves my Suzanne and I will do anything she wants because she is always right. (V, 205)

Suzanne, paint streaked on her cheeks, dressed in her short socks and flat-heeled shoes, with an old sweater and skirt, looking like a bohemian, was suspicious of Utter's smart outfits, and knew he was still longing for recognition of his own painting abilities. In 1923, she had bought a chateau in St-Bernard, near Lyon, in Utter's name. On one delightful occasion, when he took "Yvette" there, she followed them, waited until they were in bed, and locked the door for a week, sending them up boiled cabbage in a basket they lowered from their window.

Her paintings were no less uncompromising. Take the *Blue Room*, of 1923, with the large model smoking, with her blue-striped pants against a medley of patterned cloths. Oh why, lamented the critic of the Beaux-Arts for her retrospective show of paintings in Paris, at the Galerie Bernier in the summer of 1929, must she paint such "hideous shrews in tones of great vulgarity?" Why does she want to do that? Her female nudes, he said, are caricatures, and each of her flower paintings is spoiled by some detail, some basket or ladder, "placed there to look unpleasant. Does it spring from her poverty or her spite?" (V, 220)

Whitney Chadwick points out that Valadon and Modersohn-Becker were "two of the first women artists to work extensively with the nude female form. Their painting collude with, and challenge, narratives that construct female identity, through connections to nature, and that view women as controlled by emotions, sexual instincts, and biology." (Chadwick, 282) But the bohemian Valadon was seen as a "pseudo-male," and Chadwick quotes the critic Bertrand Dorival, calling her "that most virile—and greatest—of all the women in painting." Having been a model, she eschews the classically monumental nude figure and the "lush surface" for the male gaze, stressing instead the specific context and action of her frequently awkward full-bodied figures, turning away from the viewer and absorbed in what they are doing. They are sturdy, going about their business of bathing or resting, instead of connecting visually with the viewer. (Chadwick, 286)

Clearly, she was incorrigible in her strong-willed refusal to conform to anything at all of a socially pleasing nature. Not in her art or her life. Paul Petrides, invited to pose for her, would arrive at nine, and be kept waiting for two hours while she fed her pets and cleaned her brushes. But if he came later, she, furious, would refuse to paint him at all. A woman painter, was she? She hated the separation of genders in exhibitions, and even confessed, in a piece appearing the year after her death, to having inherited from Degas some of his misogynistic tendencies. ("Suzanne Valadon par elle-même," *Prométhée*, March, 1939)

Later, Utrillo married, to Valadon's despair, a calculating being called Lucie, who had no fondness for Utrillo's mother, and the terrible trio separated geographically and mentally. Lucie was good for Utrillo's fame, as was the tailor, dealer, and collector Petrides, who at this point bought up many Utrillos and created a shortage. In 1937 Utter was fifty, crippled with gout, and Suzanne would send him money. He wrote her in September of 1937 about her life and the circle of friends of which he disapproved, not without affection:

> My dear You-You,
> I am thinking of you, it's November, and do you remember it was then we met, so long ago. Yet you have remained intensely present in my spirit. But your impossible character . . . ? !! . . . Isn't that so, *terrible Maria!!* this word just to tell you that for a long time I have wanted you to know, but how? That I am luckily not seeing anyone from your sinister group, and that if I didn't come to kiss you and find out how you were it was from a major impossibility—I am better after my illness . . . a word from you would seal my happiness. To you, your André
> (Masle, 242)

Suzanne was always close to younger men, especially to the Russian Gazi Ignaghirei, who adopted her as his mother, and to Robert Le Masle, a homosexual. In a letter to the latter, she ended with the same enthusiastic flounce with which she would sign a vase: "Vive la jeunesse!" At the end of his letter, she wrote "Vive l'Amour!" She herself continued to flirt with men and women and to paint exactly as she liked. And Utter would send her such messages as the following:

> André to Suzanne with his unfailing love and his deep and respectful affection, to her who never understood that she should have been only and entirely his.
> Andre Utter. Noel, 1937 (Masle, 302)

Utter complained to the Utrillos of her "crazy pride," when she changed her mind about an exhibition he had arranged, and, to her, of her headstrong nature. She remained, gloriously in my view, a quite obstinate and so "terrible Maria!" Utter told his friends that she had permitted her son's marriage to punish him for his unfaithfulness. . . . And wrote a terrible message to her upon Utrillo's marriage: "Your presence (more or less legitimate) at the religious marriage of your son would exclude mine, and permits you at the same time to put in Neon letters a meter high your very authentic betrayal. Everyone looking at you will be thinking this." (Masle, 204) Which, among other things, prompted Maurice Utrillo to say of Utter: "I would only reproach him for having molested mother in word and deed." (V, 251) And, from the other point of view, that of Utter, Suzanne had only taught Utrillo the lesson of being as ugly in his painting as possible. (Masle, 203) Nevertheless, Utter had also made her happy, as had her son. They had also both made her miserable. In a drunken fit, Utter destroyed some of her paintings, as did her son but then so did her dogs. The innate violence of the human trio—each aggravating the attitude of the others, seems, in a certain reading, a source of the energy behind her unrelenting enthusiasm.

It was said that much later, toward the end, Suzanne Valadon became religious, however unlikely that seemed. Gazi discovered an ancient sanctuary under Montmartre, and believed it to be under the patronage of Notre-Dame-de-Montmartre. This tied up with an earlier experience of Valadon, who became a Christian. She had always said: "I am an atheist; I never go to church. However, nobody who knocks on my door for help goes away empty-handed." (V, 246)

Robert Naly, a neighbor of Utter's, was designated, he said, to keep her from picking up—as it seemed she was wont to do—one of the *clochards* or bums around the streets, taking him to bed, and sending him away the next day, perhaps with a Degas drawing. It is certain that she was publicly perceived as sexually voracious, at the shocking age of sixty. She had not been called "the mistress of Montmartre" for nothing; her senses were vitally a part of herself. Naly's own experience with her was different, and instructive: she slept little, and stayed up until all hours talking about painting, about Titian and Tintoretto and art techniques. The two stories in no way contradict each other—they both speak of that enthusiasm abounding in her. Her affections firmly included, as did those of Judith Gautier, Emily Carr, and Claude Cahun, her pet animals, her dogs (in 1924, L'Abri and La Misse, both mongrels), and her cats always, especially her beloved Raminou. Her pets were everywhere, on every sofa, bed, table, and she painted them everywhere. Love was not absent from her life at any point, and its objects included both sexes and both varieties of living things: persons and animals; and of places. She loved Montmartre, and she loved her chateau at Saint-Bernard, where instead of running water and electricity, she and Utter had cases of wine delivered, and feasted outdoors. Yes, Utrillo would be from time to time in a sanatorium, yes, the men would destroy her work from time to time, as would the dogs—but the things that mattered to her, mattered.

One photograph of Valadon sticks in my head, quite as surely as Renoir's and Puvis' and Toulouse-Lautrec's paintings of her. She is in her back yard in Montmartre, her easel in her left hand, and holding a flower painting with her right one. She is short, in an energetic pose, wearing socks and espadrilles, and a smock over her skirt. Her face is enthusiastic as she smiles at the camera and, by extension, at us. Now Suzanne Valadon is sixty-five, or sixty-six. She is described as old, small, and wrinkled, her "gray hair in a fringe, a large cloak, and a felt hat thrust over her forehead, mannish and gypsy-like." She has piercing eyes behind her glasses. When she does her own self-portrait, she portrays herself bare-breasted, with no illusions, not gorgeous like her André or his legs, but with sagging, real breasts of a sixty-five-year-old. This is not Paula Modersohn-Becker, whose young self-portrait with an amber necklace is so moving because so vulnerable. Not Paula, dying in childbirth and saying what a pity, she was just beginning to paint. This is not young beautiful Maria Valadon, so lovely that she was everyone in Montmartre's favorite model. What does she remind me of? She reminds me of pluck, of courage. One critic has described this painting as the "candid but proud reflection of a withered, desperately lonely, naked woman." (Gianadda, 21) I would describe it as a courageous painting, not about loneliness but about life.

It reminds me of nothing so much as of the young Suzanne, sliding down a banister naked, with nothing on but a mask. Except that here, there is no mask. She is just as she is. And that is what she always was. Jeanne Warnod, who lived near Suzanne described her in her later years, from a young girl's viewpoint:

> Suzanne seemed to me very tiny and very old, with her wrinkled face. . . . I was intimidated by the piercing eyes behind her glasses that seemed to look through you, and by her habit of blurting out exactly what she thought. . . . Impulsive, always ready to explode with anger, she was as extravagant in her generosity towards her friends as she was vehement in her exasperation at the unfairness of it all. (V, 216)

She exhibited as she had since 1909 in the Salon d'Automne, under her simple name Valadon, like a man, and remained under contract to Bernheim-Jeune. Her paintings were thought to combine masculine strength, even brutality, and a certain defensiveness — how not? And, at the end of her life, stricken with both diabetes and uremia, she was still painting nudes and bunches of roses, and, most movingly, a vase with roses bearing the words *"Vive la jeunesse!"* Long live youth indeed, but this kind of old age also. Downstairs were her stretchers and frames, and in her worn-out shoes, grubby dressing gown, with her strands of white hair, this might have seemed ironic. I think not.

In 1938, there was a group exhibition at the Galerie Bernier, on the rue Jacques-Callot, in which Valadon was included. Utter persuaded her to go, and Jacques Guenne of *L'Art Vivant* wrote the following description:

> She was ensconced in an armchair with a knitted hat on her head and bands of wool wrapped round her legs. Suzanne Valadon seemed tinier than usual but bent this time and quiet. When she caught a glimpse of me she called out: "Well, are you working?" Trying hard to conceal my emotion I muttered, "Like you, alas, with less joy!" "Be quiet," Valadon replied. "Work's the only thing that matters." (V, 247)

Now about a reputation, a legend, and a book. At Maurice Utrillo's funeral in November of 1955, there were 50,000 mourners. At Valadon's, in 1938, at the St. Pierre church in Montmartre, there were few, but notable ones: Pablo Picasso, André Derain, and André Utter. The original announcement had asked for a large assembly—"We ask her friends and admirers and all artists to feel it a duty to come"—and then watered it down slightly: the speakers were to be Georges Huisman, the director of the Ecole des Beaux-Arts, André Salmon, and Francis Carco of the Académie Goncourt. Edouard Herriot gave the memorial words about old Montmartre which her son had "made into a country, " and about Valadon: "the greatest light among the artists of this century." She was buried beside her mother, in Saint-Ouen.

After her death Utrillo wrote for her an enormously soupy poem entitled "For My Deceased Mother" (or then he didn't, the newspapers of the time are full of accusations about the fake). It goes like this, unbelievably:

> Créature d'Elite et de Bonté imbue
> En ce monde elle fut l'âpre vérité nue
> Lors, prodiguant le Bien d'un sur discernement
> Aux humbles accordant son parfait dévouement.
>
> Le Dieu Suprême enfin de l'Eclatante nue
> Lui donna en apport sa naissance venue
> Ce don divin de l'Art, toutes choses, retraçant
> En infaillibles traits du Pinceau enchantant.
>
> Las le Sort fut cruel à l'Ame disparue
> Qui de mille tourments fut la proie ingénue
> Me chérissant toujours de son doux coeur aimant.

En ce jour d'Avril tendre à sa fin las venue
Je déplorai du ciel cette Loi inconnue
Emportant ici-bas bonheur en un instant.

> Maurice Utrillo
> (Masle, Utrillo papers, 49)

Chosen being, imbued with goodness,
In this world she was the harsh naked truth
When, offering the gift of a sure perception
She granted to the humble her perfect devotion.

In fact the Supreme God of the Shining cloud
Bestowed on her at birth
This divine gift of Art, all things, retracing
In infallible strokes of the enchanting Brush.

Alas Fate was cruel to the vanished Soul
The naive prey of a thousand torments
Always caring for me with her sweet loving heart.

In this tender April day alas come to her end
I deplored this mysterious Law
Snatching away our joy in an instant.

And Utrillo left us a letter, equally soupy: "a letter to My Mother: Oh my mother! All self-sacrifice and goodness, charitable soul above any other. . . ." What to say?

About R.J. Boulan's work called "Utrillo's Love Story," concocted mostly by Utrillo's wife Lucie, Picasso and Derain protested to Utrillo himself in the journal of the *Beaux-Arts*, November 18, 1938, calling it a "tissue of lies." It was composed of fantastic episodes, with Lucie as the heroine, brought by the fairies to Utrillo. And in it Valadon was simply referred to as the "gifted mother of a genius, whose name would become as well-known as her son's." Indeed. She had more gifts than is sometimes allowed. I want to end on her most extraordinary gift, that of courage.

Two things, among many others, perfectly illustrate this. In 1936, Suzanne Valadon had painted a vase with the inscription *Vive la Jeunesse*, in a picture now given this title and referred to above. And second, I think about the figure of the young André Utter, half her age, and gorgeous, and whose figure she portrays in the epic fishing scene called *The Casting of the Net*. This strong painting was inspired by the fishermen of Corsica where, in 1913, the "terrible trio" were together. But the legs therein are those of Utter, and they recur in the extraordinary still life of 1923, entitled *Still Life with a Violin Case*, behind the table. Thus one painting is recalled another. The legs might be mistaken at first glance for the trees in a forest, so that the "legs" and "trees" of her autobiographical "Suzanne ou l'absolu" find their fulfillment here. "I would have wished to . . . show, so that I could keep: trees, legs —certainly I could ask that of the gods." (Masle) So the *Still Life* brings back at once the earlier romance which, indeed, she kept, and her writing, in a double memory. This is then a canvas remembering and to be remembered, although in many reproductions, the legs are cropped out of the picture, as something extraneous. To be sure, Utter left her later, and things went bad. But they never divorced, and her still life remained to refresh the epic memory. It will always remain like that, in a sort of Proustian recall.

Above all, Valadon could surely claim a fidelity to herself in all her eccentric strongwilledness: "My work . . . is finished," she said to Francis Carco, "and the only satisfaction I gain from it is that I have never surrendered. I have never betrayed anything that I believed in." (V, 1) What she also believed was that we would know it in the future, "if anyone cares to do me justice." There has been a lot of caring, about her ceaseless war against the values of a bourgeois society, about her work ethic, about her painting and her life. I hope to have done her justice.

In 1937, Valadon, now seventy-one, had gone to an exhibition of European women painters at the Jeu de Paume, which included Berthe Morisot and Marie Laurencin and herself. Never one to underrate herself, luckily, Valadon said to her friend alongside her: "do you know, chérie, I think perhaps God has made me France's greatest woman painter." (V, 244)

"Work's the only thing that matters." Valadon had a stroke at seventy-three, and died at her easel, on April 7, 1938. How could this be other than a witness to the true painter's truest calling?

CHAPTER 3

DOROTHY BUSSY

TRANSLATING A PASSION

Dear Gide, I could go on talking to you for ever. You seem to me some-times the only person I can talk to about everything.

—*Dorothy Bussy, seventy-nine, to André Gide, seventy-six,*
October 30, 1944

Just imagine the story. A daughter of the wealthy, numerous, and famously intelligent Strachey family—Lytton's sister Dorothy—nurses back to health Simon Bussy, a penniless French painter studying in London, who has been introduced by Auguste Bréal, one of Simon's fellow students at the Ecole-des Beaux-Arts in Paris. She marries the slightly younger Simon, and they go to live in a small and enchanting house, La Souco, in Roquebrune near Menton, high above the sea and nestled in a garden of flowers, described by Lytton as a tiny Paradise of three inches square. An expert on languages (with her own program on the BBC about the teaching of English) and a translator, she converses with her husband in English, and he, speaking no English, responds in French.

During one of their yearly visits to her family in England, André Gide, accompanied by his young lover Marc Allégret, and desirous of learning English, is introduced to the Bussys, again by Bréal. When Dorothy returns to France, they correspond, she writing him in English, he responding in French, in order, he says, to get his precise meaning across. This is a peculiar echo of her linguistic relation to her husband. Dorothy becomes his translator, first of *Strait is the Gate* (*La Porte étroite*), and later of his other works, and falls in love with him, even as she is aware of his homosexual leanings. These were not only acknowledged but an important part of his writing life and public persona, about which he deeply cared: witness *Corydon* and *Si le grain ne meurt (Lest it Die)*.

The impossibility of her love might be seen, or translated, as an essential component of her fervent adoration. As Gide's biographer, Alan Sheridan, describes it succinctly: "She fell instantly, passionately in love with Gide. At fifty-three, a plain, bespectacled lady, four years older than Gide, she had everything against her, but her passion endured to the end." (Sheridan, xiv) In her unpublished journal, which she and Gide called her "black notebook," she recounts her passionate daydreams as well as his personal confessions about his marriage and loves and attraction to young boys, and recounts the best as well as the most difficult times of their relation. Strangely unproblematic was Simon's attitude to the whole thing occurring so close to him: sublimely unaware or remarkably understanding, he lived in another world altogether. "Simon never reads your letters. He understands," says Dorothy to Gide. (*Letters*, xv) We don't know, of course, exactly what he understood or how he measured his wife's affections.

Gide admired Simon's paintings and watercolors, some of which he acquired, and for which he arranged exhibitions and wrote encouraging reviews and recommendations. Simon's world and art were populated largely by animals, although his portraits of their friends, André Gide, Paul Valéry, Roger Martin du Gard, John Maynard Keynes, Ottoline Morrell (with green hair), and his wife Dorothy, seated rather primly, in a white collar and black dress, are well known. He spent his time drawing at the zoo when they were in Paris or London, and seemed, in his daily life at home, to be somewhere else always, according to the accounts of every visitor to La Souco.

The Bussys, always impoverished, took in paying guests ("P.G." in the letters and notebooks), among whom one of the most frequent was Gide, causing anguish and delight to Dorothy, who was always wishing he would linger after dinner so they could be alone, or longing to tap on his door to be comforted about his sometimes apparent coldness in such proximity to the heat of her fantasy.

This mingling of three creators in their own world and language is nothing short of remarkable. Dorothy has often been ridiculed for her "absurd" attraction to a man taken up with his own kind, and her husband, for not having seen what was going on in his own wife's mind. But in fact, said Dorothy to Gide, Simon was simply not interested, neither in her letters from him (after all, Simon had his own letters), nor in her emotions toward this family friend, so that the latter were channeled into her private writing, vivid, dramatic, and haunted.

The reader follows the ups and downs of her passion and the intricacies of her smallest gestures that speak so loudly: she would rest her hand for an instant on Gide's hand, in which he held some book he was reading to her. She would long to kiss it, but did not. She would kiss the lapel of his coat, not his lips. She would commit and repent her "indiscretions" in writing a letter to him, would mail it, then rush to write another to undo the effect of the first.

The years between 1920 and 1924 were full of her recriminations, complaints, and anguish. Nevertheless, her denials were many, of such feelings as she clearly had. Mme Théo van Rysselberghe—"La Petite Dame," the mother of Elizabeth with whom André Gide had his daughter, Catherine—recounts, on September 14, 1920, in her journal (modestly entitled "Notes pour l'histoire authentique d'André Gide," or, notes for his authentic story [!]), that Dorothy had said to him, "You don't know anything about passion, you just love people for what they represent." And she recounts that he replied "Yes, there's something true about that." (Cahiers Petite Dame, 46) On December 6 of the same year, she writes that Gide had received a burningly impassioned letter from her, which he found "admirable," and that their conversation then turned, full of "choses charmantes" (!) around his reflection: "I am very thankful to the gods not to have any passion for you."

Because, he said, "that would be immediately intolerable, and so much less amusing!" (Cahiers Petite Dame, 64) A note points out, as if any reader would need such clarification, that "Dorothy Bussy had conceived a lively passion for Gide" and points to her correspondence with him.

In July of 1921, Dorothy wrote:

> I don't think you have any *real interest* in me. Why—or how—in Heaven's name should you?
> Not a saint—not a boy—just your hopeless and yet not altogether unhappy
> Lover D.B. (*Letters*, 74)

Yet barely two months later, she exclaimed how horrid he was to her: "Horrid—horrid . . . I always said to myself if he dislikes me for what I *am*, too bad, tant pis, there's nothing to be done." (October 3, 1921, *Letters*, 74-5) Her anguish increased with her love. Her situation she understood completely, lucidly, even as she overstated every case, insisting "you never cared for me," inciting his reply, which she probably expected, that she preferred to tear herself apart like a wave against the rock, blaming the rock for the pain, while it is simply "firm and constant." In short, her silence would have perhaps been better for her peace of mind, had she craved that—yet from her passionate outpourings, albeit too close for any ease, Gide admitted he had learned much. At eighty-two, in the month before he died, he wrote to Dorothy, now eighty-five, "On the whole I already knew, thanks to you, so many things. Then there are others that I sense so well!" (January 9, 1951)

In the Bloomsbury group, to which Dorothy Strachey Bussy was connected by her Strachey blood, these intimate and seemingly unbalanced relations of a woman and a homosexual man were part of a noticeable pattern. Dorothy's own singular relation to Gide during her marriage to Simon strikes the reader of letters and lives as not dissimilar to Vanessa Bell's lifelong attachment to Duncan Grant, during her marriage to Clive Bell, or Carrington's to Lytton Strachey, during her marriage to Ralph Partridge. Dorothy once exclaimed, on a visit to Ham Spray, which Carrington had decorated for Lytton Strachey, and where they lived: "a pathetic ménage if ever there was one. So much adoration on one side, so much affection on the other—and the whole thing hopelessly unsuitable." (October 31, 1918, *Letters*, 4). The passage is ironic in the light of Dorothy's own future.

In my view, neither the various household arrangements nor the various emotional involvements were unsuitable, for, despite the anguish, *they worked*. In each case, a strong-minded and artistically oriented woman, married to a heterosexual man, remained in her most important relation with a man oriented toward other men. In each case, it was the singular and "inappropriate," thus eccentric, relation that lasted as the crucial one, for the work and the life of both beloved and loving—each dependent upon the other. We have only to reread these letters between Dorothy and the man she spent her life loving and translating to see the essential nature of the relation between them. These three beloved men, all extraordinary, all homosexual, were able, for all the pain caused by the inbalance of their relations, to nourish the mind and work of the imaginative and strong personalities that these women were. We too have to make a true reading as best we can.

In many works about Gide, including Albert Guerard's anthology of essays about him, published by Harvard in 1969, there is absolutely no mention of Dorothy Bussy. In Sheridan's recent biography, where her role is definitely both a minor and an unthankful one, she is relegated, along with his secretary Yvonne Davet, to the role of an adorer—yes, she translated him, of course, but that is about it. My contention is that for all her knowledge of his unavailability, it was all the same her passion for him that gave her work its flair and her life its meaning. This is no small thing.

Moreover, we should not overlook how Gide's affections grew, unlike what is usually thought of him. On January 22, 1946, he wrote from Cairo: "I don't think about anything. . . . My life is only near you, with you—and all your amiable pessimism doesn't prevent you from knowing it." (*Letters*, 246) On February 2, 1948: "I think of you constantly"; and on March 8 of the same year: "How much there is to say to you!" (*Letters*, 276, 281)

Simon the painter translated his beloved animals into his art; his wife translated one of France's greatest writers from his language into hers. Both the Bussys left, discreetly, these most important relations in their own language, unshared by the other. And, of course, the letters between Gide and Dorothy are also in two languages. Notably unusual relations, such as those between this creative threesome, hold an incontrovertible fascination. Each of these literary and personal relations and their expressions—translations, all of them—is inimitable, intimately indescribable except in its own language. Whatever interpretation we make is already a translation, another one.

To the published selections, both in English and in French, of the letters exchanged between Dorothy and Gide, an epilogue by Roger Martin du Gard has been added. He had always served as a sort of go-between, being Gide's closest friend and someone in whom, in principle, both Dorothy and Gide had confidence. On May 25, 1949, he added a note to a bundle of papers from which the published letters have been taken. In it he describes how Madame Simon Bussy had given him a batch of papers (the "black notebook") a few days earlier, on May 11, 1949, to show to Gide, who was in the clinic in Nice, and then to keep. Gide, once back in Paris, had added to them some separate pages she had sent him as Dorothy had wished him to do.

In Martin du Gard's note, he recounts the scene when he gave the envelope to Gide in the clinic, which he did on May 23. As he remembered it, Gide said to him:

> This love of Dorothy's has been a pathetic thing. There are some overwhelming passages in these notes, overwhelming to me, and for any reader. . . . And by depositing these papers in your archives, Dorothy certainly hopes they will one day be exhumed. There is an astonishing page where she tells herself that she has been, in my life, the only

woman who might have been the cause of my "infidelity"—of my
infidelity vis-a-vis my wife, and that is why she frightened me, why I
protected myself against her love. . . .

She seems to have thought, said Gide, that had she mattered less, she
might have obtained more. Martin du Gard had interrupted him at
this point, saying: "Fortunate illusion . . . in which she likely found
her one consolation!" Then Gide, said Martin du Gard,

> made a gesture of vague hesitation, as though he were not aware that
> Dorothy deluded herself, quite willing *perhaps to* accept, retrospectively,
> this psychological subtlety, precisely because of its subtlety. But I who
> have heard his confidences concerning Dorothy since 1920 and in the
> following years, I remember with no possible error that he never felt
> for her more than a compassionate and deeply tender friendship, that
> he was always incapable of returning any of that frenetic passion she
> felt for him, that he avoided her, fled from her, so as not to have to
> repulse her and cause her too much pain . . .

Then, says Martin du Gard, Gide said to him: "You cannot imagine,
dear, what attraction I feel for her face, and always more so, truly,
with the years. . . . I look at her now, with more emotion than ever."
(*Letters*, 307) And about the whole packet, said Gide, including
her subsequent papers sent to him: "It will form an ensemble, which
will have some interest perhaps, later on." (*Letters*, 306-7) Indeed it
does, now.

Of course this is Roger Martin du Gard's own rendering of
Gide's recountings and of his gesture, just as Dorothy's rendering
of conversations and gestures in her letters and notes is her own.
Readers will have their own judgments about the texts and the situations. It is perhaps unnecessary to point out many of the judgments of the outside world, in addition to Martin du Gard's: I will
let the example of Gide's more recent biographer stand as exem-
plary. He is of course right in describing Dorothy as "poor
Dorothy . . . accustomed to rejection" (Sheridan, 341) and her
over-the-top expressions of passion are indeed embarrassing, such
as the one he quotes after that description: "In a final, ill-chosen
metaphor, she became Mary Magdalen, pouring 'my box of
ointment over your feet'." Later, he points out how "the poor
woman was as much as ever at sea about the emotional as well
as the sexual promiscuity of her soul's idol." (Sheridan, 360)
"Reading such effusions," he says, "it is hard to remember that this

is a sixty-four-year-old woman addressing a sixty-year-old man."
(Sheridan, 433) Gide's other obsessive adorer, Yvonne Davet, his
secretary whom Gide had asked Dorothy to look after, had her
own "Gidean hell" to deal with, for he was clearly attractive to
women, sometimes "with tumultuous results: in both cases, Gide
displayed endless endurance and patience. Any other man would
have got rid of them at the outset." (Sheridan, 625).

Yet I have chosen to quote at length from Dorothy's unpublished
"black notebook" and papers, which she gave Martin du Gard and
those she sent Gide. It seems to me important to give Dorothy's
point of view, and her remembrances of Gide, which can then be
interpreted by subsequent readers. I am necessarily making my own.

In the reading of letters and journals, it is urgent to follow the
plot line, particularly in this case, with Gide so secretive and
Dorothy so unsecretive, in letters, in the pages of her black notebook, which she wanted Gide to see, and in the other pages she
sent Gide and wanted placed alongside the first ones. I have done
my best with the dates, for many entries are undated. These are
pages of writing, not just of telling, and she clearly wanted them
read, as did Gide. There are passages in pencil, and in ink, passages
crossed out and writ large, passages that break off, as if the thought
had been unbearable to contemplate. Perhaps so.

The placing of this epilogue by Martin du Gard—who, Dorothy
points out, is "bad about women" (*Letters*, 166)—after the letters
leaves its own heavy mark on the tale. I feel it important to cite, as
I think both the characters in this drama would have approved,
Gide's statement on April 26, 1921, about Dorothy's "black notebook"—he, as the keeper of a journal he would eventually publish,
urged her to keep up hers, as her account of their relationship:
"Out of pity for both of us, Oh don't give up writing to me . . . and
don't give up writing the account you have begun either. If you
agree to believe me, I will agree to tell you that I think of you very
often." (*Letters*, 68) She did not give it up, and believed him,
despite the melodramatic ups and downs in that relationship, for
the rest of their long lives. Gide was to die in 1951, and Dorothy, in
1960.

A few odd details emerge that throw light on the unpublished doc-
uments. One is that Knopf, the publishers, were most unenthusiastic
about Dorothy's translations and urged Gide to find another translator. This he did not do, except for his brief tale *Thésée*, feeling in
this case that a deep masculine voice was needed.

In their lengthy discussions about their reading of Dostoevsky and others, and about Gide's translations of Shakespeare, notably *King Lear* and *Hamlet*, Gide's respect for Dorothy's judgment was clear, and their interchange is of especial fascination. Here is a typical letter, from Dorothy, written in 1950, long after her passion for Gide had somewhat calmed down, and after their shared intellectual exchange had continued for so long. Dorothy could hold her own with Gide, as she had proved many times over, and here again. Gide has been lacking in what she considers proper respect for Lear:

Tuesday April 5 1950
Please forgive this further outcry about King Lear. I do want you to reconsider your judgment. I would like you—oh! so much! to reconsider it in writing. I am afraid that with your immense authority you may lead astray whole generations of young Frenchmen into misjudging a work which really deserves a little more respect than you give it.
. . .

Of course Lear is "senile, silly, stupid." That is where the whole point of the work lies. He impersonates the luxury, folly, indifference and selfishness of the wealthy and powerful, who have never come into contact with reality and who are suddenly forced to experience all its horrors. His sufferings are caused partly by his own folly and intemperance, partly by the crimes of others and partly by the ferocity of the Gods in Heaven and by the senseless, overpowering forces of Nature. Shakespeare is not trying to be human here; he doesn't want (unless incidentally) to move us to pity or to wring our "intestines." His subject is more than that. "Enormous," you say with scorn. "Factitious and false"! What work of art is not? Must men then never be ambitious? Must they never even attempt greatness? At one stroke you would abolish The Book of Job, Prometheus Bound, Paradise Lost, and Dostoievski's novels. The "breathtaking" temple of Abu Simbel too . . . that such works can never have the quality of perfection is more than likely. I do not claim it for Shakespeare—neither here nor anywhere else—and it is perhaps a pity that his only available tool was the drama, which, I expect, requires *perfection* more than any other form of art, and which enabled you to compare him (the final insult) with Victor Hugo!

You complain too that all the characters, good and bad alike, are confounded at the end in an indifferent hecatomb. What other end was possible to such a subject? Would you, like the 18th century, have preferred Edgar and Cordelia to make a happy marriage and live happily ever after? Shakespeare, at any rate sometimes, was able to resist the snare of a happy ending.

There are other things too which one might have thought would appeal to you. That kind of prefiguring and redoubling of incidents, which you admire in Hamlet and, I believe, in other cases too, here you brush away contemptuously. In spite of your friends Tiresias and Oedipus, you see nothing suggestive in the fact that it is only when Gloucester's eyes are put out that he sees the truth. The questions of bastardy, of adultery, of men and women's sensual behaviour, which Lear harps upon have apparently no interest for you, though they seem to be treated with some originality. . . .

Shakespeare, no doubt, almost recovered from his nervous *breakdown*. In his last three plays (the Winter's Tale, Cymbeline and the Tempest), he has more or less climbed out of his pit. Not altogether, though. For there too we find the wicked violence of Leontes, the imprecations of Pauline, the monstrosities of Clote and Caliban. But he has consented in these, as he did not for Cordelia, to bestow a final and lovely happiness on Perdita, Imogen, and Ariel. And you must be hard-hearted indeed, if you do not find in Cordelia's first meeting with Lear after the break, and her death in his arms, the most exquisite, the purest, the divinest poetry. (*Letters*, 294)

Gide was not hard-hearted, did recognize poetry when he heard or saw it, and was right about Thésée's voice. For indeed, Dorothy was finally persuaded about her not being the appropriate voice for Gide's *Thésée*, whose character she greatly disliked, finding neither any agreeable women in the tale whose voice she would have liked to speak in. However she claimed, rightly, that her judgment of English translations was superior to most critics, including Mrs. Knopf. In fact, as she wrote on May 11, 1946, "I will tell you that the infinite patience and conscientiousness and fidelity that is necessary in a translator is more often found among women." Men, she said, as a rule prefer to work for themselves, not in a subordinate role. (*Letters*, 250)

Now there is no getting around it: on the sentimental level, Dorothy's letters are clearly excruciating, for Gide and for the reader, in their adoration. She does not dare to try to "penetrate his mystery." It is quite like Judith Gautier's worshipful attitude toward Wagner. This early letter of June 16, 1919, refers, as many of her letters do, to Shakespeare, in this case, *Hamlet*:

Would I seem to know your stops? Would I pluck out the heart of your mystery?. Never—never. God forbid! . . . I know that the darkness through which your light shines is you as much as the light. I don't want the darkness gone—only to come near to it—as near as I dare and you will let me. And sometimes I tremble to think how strangely, unexpectedly near I am

. . .

> Oh! Gide—How do I dare? How do I dare write to you? Why do you encourage it? You could easily stop me, you know. When you say it's time to go, I don't wait to be told twice, do I? (*Letters*, 25)

Oof. No, he did not try to stop her altogether, and she did dare, finding the writing torture, and then, writing another letter to undo the first, a habit that Gide would treat gently, if mockingly. In 1919, she was not yet keeping a diary, but soon would, about their relation, about their meetings, about her feelings.

In the meantime, there were her letters, many, many of them: Gide had been speaking of his "profound friendship" for her, and she replied, on October 18, 1919:

> As for me, I should hardly dare call the feeling that I have for you profound. How could it be, with no roots in the past and no hopes for the future? And faithful? OH! that's a word I gave up using long years ago. But it's acute, it's sometimes even agonising. It's a continual longing to see you again. It's a desperate curiosity for everything that concerns you . It's a constant dreaming of your face and voice. It's an aching desire to expend myself somehow or other in some kind of vain and useless sacrifice for you—for you—And it's complicated by the horrid knowledge of how old I am, of how little right I have to have such feelings and how unfit I am in every way to be your friend. No equality, no communion seems henceforth possible. I have *no* advantages. I am even only half intelligent. And I have probably by all this for ever destroyed what was pleasant between us—the "camaraderie" of the Cambridge days. Oh! happy Cambridge days, when I was just your dictionary and your grammar, convenient and helpful. And you had the same kind of friendly feeling for me that one has for a dictionary. I understood *that* perfectly. And you didn't notice—you were too much engrossed by other things—that your dictionary had eyes and a heart, was watching you and wondering at you, was charmed and thrilled and shaken by you. . . . Aren't you the strangest and the loveliest and the most disturbing thing I have ever come across in my life? Oh! happy days, when I could love you safely and comfortably without your knowing it, without knowing it myself. . . .

And, a few days later, predictably, arrived her regret about "that last foolish letter of mine. . . . A letter always arrives too late—one can never catch it up—and this too will be wrong by the time it reaches you." (*Letters*, 35–36)

Over and over, Gide would meditate with Dorothy, in his conversations and letters, about his relation to his wife Madeleine—already a rather odd conversation, given Dorothy's adoration. But, of course, she felt privileged to hear his ruminations and notes them down at excruciating length. He would speak of his love for Madeline, how his life was centered around her, and yet how living with her was anguishing, how he could not work and how, specifically, the temptation for him at Cuverville was intense: the young boys in the neighborhood, of course.

> How can I work? And yet I have to, or it will be the end of everything. And then the kind of temptation there is for me is particularly dangerous—if I let myself succumb to it, it will be awful—awful for her. So the only thing to do is not to go out at all.
>
> Oh, she is afraid of me . . . She's quite *right* to be afraid. I am *dangerous*. . . . nearby is a family with young people—a child of 12 or 13. What anguish for her! To say nothing of anyone's feelings, what a scandal ! not that anything very serious goes on there. Don't think it does . . . but I am so thirsty for youth. . . . such a need to surround myself with everything young and laughing. But I think I can manage not to go there any more, yes, I believe I have that strength . . . After all, I'm not thirty any more.
>
> And then, what to do? Ask her to accompany me to Italy when I know what will happen there, and the first little kid I see in the street. . . . Ah no, no! I know myself! *I know myself.*

What to do? And Gide worried even more about his double desire: wanting to leave with Marc on a pleasure trip, but wanting to reassure Madeleine. In Dorothy he had an eager listener: everything that concerned him concerned her. On and on he went, about Madeleine's understanding his relation to Marc better . . . Wishful thinking: . . . and then, said Dorothy,

> I said the only word I said during the whole of this soliloquy: "That's why she looks happy."
> He repeated it two or three times: "Yes, that's why she looks so happy . . ."

Dorothy had just met Madeleine, and found her agreeable enough. But, on the topic of separateness, Gide continued:

> "She has *cut me out* of her life. I feel that she wants to separate from me, absolutely. Knowing that I have chosen that dangerous path, she doesn't want to encourage me in it. She doesn't want to take that responsibility. She wants me to be alone.
>
> —Say something to her? No, no. I am physically incapable of it. My heart is beating too violently. It would kill me. And then what's the

use? No, no. Silence is better. Yes, silence will be better. Yes, silence will end by becoming eloquent.

At one point, Madeleine had come home, and Marc had been sleeping there: "Only you can understand that, that's why I always speak to you about it." Dorothy continued about herself: "I have never been nearer his tragedy. With what a foolish little line do I try to sound these depths. Oh, no! God forbid that I should try! But how easily I rest upon the surface, delight in the gentleness and gaiety of the surface—and forget the horror, the violence of what is below." About her own relation to him and her expression of it, she remained lucid: Ah, too much, too often, with too little restraint, she said of her letters. Ah, if she were only young and beautiful . . . Gide had expressed his surprise at "the resources of her heart . . ."

With all the ups and downs of their epistolary and psychological relation, as *written* as it is felt, readers are likely either to be intrigued or exasperated, just like Gide. They were both readers, as well as writers, as is evident. She *stages* her emotions and his: He has nothing at all to say to her? What can she say? Her resentment? She has no right. Her pity? It irritates him. "My love? Zut! Assez!—My affection?—I don't feel it today. My disgust for myself.—A disgusting subject—What then? Nothing—nothing." This letter, on May 22, 1921, had no address, as she said, on purpose. (*Letters*, 69)

In the "black book," Dorothy observes Gide's every move, from the beginning—he looks so tired:

> Nov. 15, 1921 But no! that impression didn't last longer than the first evening. I thought afterwards that he looked tired with a fatigue that wasn't merely physical. There was something discouraged about his mouth—as if he were beginning to taste the bitterness of life. When he ran there was less lightness, when he laughed less bouyancy.

And so the saga continued, Gide feeling burdened by Dorothy's excessive affection, not wanting to put her off but also unable to respond as she would have chosen. His solution was never to reply to her letters exactly, as he points out to her; and, when they were alone at Roquebrune, he would just read quietly to himself, or read aloud to her, a good moment for both of them:

March 25th (1922)
This afternoon we went and sat under the olive trees and he read me some more of *Si le grain ne meurt*: the part about Lord A[lfred]

D[ouglas]. about his leaving Algeria, about his good-bye to Athman. And then he talked. He told me he had wondered how he would finish the book but that now he knew what the natural, logical end of it would be. It would end with his mother's death and then he would write no more of his recollections.

He said that he was afraid people would think he had had impure relations with Athman. It would be absurd to say that he hadn't in the book, but as a matter of fact he hadn't—such an idea was horrible, impossible, a sacrilege. He had tried to convey this, he hoped he had.

Over and over they would discuss Marc's love for Gide: was it as Gide would have liked it to be?

It was then I think that he said, alluding to a phrase in his Memoir: "Every obstacle in my life has only been a delay to what I desired . . . . never stopped it. That sometimes terrifies me to think that everything I want I get . . . as if I had a *demoniacal* power. . . .

"Marc's little brother: there's a child I love and who loves me, I feel it. It hurts me, because I can't do anything for him. I love him a great deal—and there it is. Life will necessarily put a distance between us."

That was a happy afternoon. I felt him happy to be with me. In spite of himself the atmosphere of my emotion excites him; he lets himself go to it as he does to the warmth, the sun, the spring. My affection "*le gonfle.*" (That is a word he is fond of.)

As for her feeling, Dorothy says she has "always been able to love more than I have been loved . . . without suffering from it." (Fortunate Dorothy, we think, before rushing into judgment about masochistic tendencies. Actually, I think Gide was rather fortunate also, to have such a willing listener and transcriber.)

Sun 27 (1922)
He often says to me: "You love to torment yourself." And I answer "No, I see the truth." "The truth if you like, but you give it the color you wish."

She recounts all their meetings like a drama: and of course, to her, they were just that. In Paris, they meet. Sometimes, all is joyous:

In the evening he came to see us at our hotel, and stayed talking for an hour. His charming talk! Gay and sweet and easy! Wanting to please—happy to please!

I don't know whether it is that I am getting to know him better, but every time I see him now, he seems to me more *powerful*. No, when I knew him first I didn't find him powerful. Ardent, eager, *avid*, greedy—but for himself. I mean the fire in him burnt for himself more than it was given out to others. Yes, that is it. He was still assimilating—now he is beginning to triumph.

As she transcribes their interchange at length, the reader is constantly surprised at her bravery in her unreciprocated devotion.

> May 3, Paris 1922
> I: Can't you tell me from time to time that I'm right to keep on sending   you letters?
> He: You have to write me, you have to. It's your duty. As much as I   hate duties, I respect duty. I am a man who sees that.
> I: But do you understand that it takes a certain heroism to do it?
> He: Yes, yes.
> I: Provided you realize that.
> He: Yes, yes, I realize it. That's why your letters are so . . . [stops there].

Yes, he stops there, but we are (I trust) astonished at his conceit and anousal of it:

> "It's a terrible thing to say, but I am no longer modest. (And he smiled.) I have no modesty left. I know I am important. I *feel myself important*." He said it smilingly, but he was in earnest. There was no trace of boasting in it, he said it with a kind of intimate conviction—a kind of astonished pride . . . no, no, none of that gives an idea of how he said it. He said it as it should be said. "I am horribly tired. I have worked so much this winter. I love that—I love working," and then in a whisper, "I'm afraid I like work more than pleasure. . . . It's awful!"
> . . . .
> And again, "I have worked so much this winter; I am exhausted, and haven't slept for several nights. That's bad. I'm terribly afraid of becoming feeble-minded. After the Immoralist, I stayed seven years without being able to write one word; if that should happen to me now, it would be the end."

It was then a question of whether or not he should publish his memoirs. Ah no, said Dorothy, but Gide insisted that he should,

> "Because every single reason I have not to publish them is a reason of cowardice. My wife? The pain I will give her? What do you expect? Do you think it is possible to do anything at all without hurting someone? Every important act necessarily hurts someone. I'm not speaking of myself any more. . . . but Christ, didn't he hurt his parents terribly?"
> . . . ."Is it from a thirst for martyrdom that you want to publish them?"
> . . . . "No, no, it's from a horror of lying—especially in marriage." (This in a whisper.)

Dorothy's interpretations are at once accurate and generous to a fault:

> It is true that he is elusive—*insaisissable*. He hates to be caught, to be bound by anything—by feelings or thoughts—by the past or by the future. He never makes a promise or an engagement frankly without leaving himself some loophole, some means of escape—lest the constraint should be intolerable to his mind or his heart, or just simply to the humour of the moment. And so it seems often that he promises more than he performs. *Disappointing?* Yes, afraid of compromising himself—not vis-a-vis of the opinions of the world but vis-a-vis of himself. He wants to be, as he says, *available* entirely and at every moment of his life. (But a fortune that is always *available* is even more useless than one that is disposed of.)
>
> He never *wants* to hurt like a coquette, for the pleasure of hurting—for the pleasure of feeling his own power. But he doesn't *mind* hurting—he will hurt remorselessly for an *end*.

This insistence of Gide on publishing his intimate memoirs, and Dorothy's analysis of his character in relation to his giving pain will be of significance later, when it is her turn to be desperately wounded by his outspokenness.

In her letters, Dorothy insists: she will write anything at all that she chooses. But her correspondence and her journal are always full of hesitations: "Was there ever a more ludicrous correspondence than ours?" June 5, 1922, Letters, 85.

She describes the fateful meeting at Pontigny, in August of 1923. Gide told her than of his being about to have a baby with Elizabeth von Rysselberghe, who, like Gide, had wanted a child).

And they had discussed despair:

> "Do you often think about death?" he asked.
> "All the time."
> "All the time. How odd," he murmured. "For me, I often feel already dead. I see myself acting like a ghost. Everything seems to me far away—so vague-in—such an atmosphere of fog. It's not me any longer living. It's my ghost."
> Was it a contradiction when he said a few minutes later, "I don't think I am aging. I don't manage to age; everything calls me—everything excites me, as if I were young. I have just as many desires, as many instincts. I don't think about squelching them—however there are far fewer occasions to satisfy them."
> And then again we walked up the dark avenue and in the middle in the darkest part he stopped and kissed me good bye. One of those

kisses he gives me as a duty—a kiss on my forehead—and he offered me his cheek—put his cheek against my lips. But my lips were as cold as his cheek. They didn't move as they touched it. I seemed to be frozen to my marrow.

We are frozen in our fascination: What a scene!

"You never know what might happen, but I imagine that after we are dead, it could get quite interesting. People know me so little. They judge me so wrongly. The impression they have of me is so different from the way it really is. I would like for the truth to be known some day.
"What do people think of you?"
"That I am a dry-hearted person. That I am intelligent, very intelligent—as much talent as anyone could wish—but *nothing* else. Emptiness. Instead of 'nature abhors a vacuum,' they said it of me. Because I have no history with women . . . like the others . . . they think I don't feel anything . . . that I am nothing."

Dorothy insists on the importance of the interchange they are having, and how he is right that it should be noted down, since she will be almost invisible in the dramatic dialogue that will read like a Gidean monologue: "Oh, keep on, please, keep on—keep on. I think it isn't only either that it is me that it interests. I think it will be interesting like the paintings of Gorki. To see the face change as you know it better . . . and then the other character . . . you. I try to suppress myself as much as possible." She puts the following sentence in ink, after the penciled passages above, and after it, returns to her normal penciled transcription: "I am with you as I am with no one else . . . noone," he said. And now the following, in pencil:

And so no one will ever know *or imagine* [*crossed out*] what he was with me. But *I* know that the unimaginable loveliness of his face & voice were no illusion of mine. His soul looked at me spoke tome. *I recognized its beauty in my heart* [*crossed out*]
And he said to me "Don't leave me, say it. You won't leave me?" . . . But I don't think he meant a *voluntary* leaving.

Gide continues to comment on his marriage. Dorothy is bound to feel complimented:

"And she—perhaps it is a paradox . . . but I am swimming in paradox . . . since my birth . . . it's even a paradox that I am saying all this to you . . . but she—it's a passion she has for *both of us* at once. How to explain that? I think she loves him—and me too—him because of me and me because of him.—And me? My feelings? I have great gratitude to her and much tenderness—but no love at all. It doesn't feel indecent

for me to talk to you about it. It's so far from me that I have been almost astonished to see the effect it has on you." [crossed out]
. . . .
"And yet it would be unworthy of you if I didn't talk to you about it. Even it if hurts you, I have to be able to talk with you about it . . . otherwise it would be unworthy of you."
He repeated that two or three times. Oh! when have I refused to listen to him? To what have I not listened? Have I ever shrunk from listening?

Again he started discussing how he must publish his memoirs, so as not to be "diminished" in her and Martin du Gard's eyes, as if he had feared the disapproval of the public. And asked her to let him recite once more Keats's "Ode to a Nightingale" to correct his pronunciation. A perfect scene, for both of them:

He put his arm through mine & we walked up & down as he repeated it—in that same sweet low trembling voice, which was the first thing I fell in love with, and once his voice faltered & broke. "I don't have a voice any more, he said." "It's all the feeling." And we looked at each other & then when it was over he said "I have to leave soon— in fifteen minutes" and I should be plunged again into my exile which seems more intolerable because there is no communication with him whatever—it is a total extinction of light.

More discussion of their exchange of letters — should she not write him?

And then he begged me:
"Don't doubt me. Don't go away from me. You haven't the right."
"Sometimes," I said, and it is true, "it seems to me that I am more separated from you than ever!"
"Ah, no!"
"You don't want me to love you any longer."
"Nonsense, nonsense," he said in English . . . "it is nonsense."
"You don't want me to say it to you any more."
"Nonsense."

The dramatic dialogue she works out appeals to the high intensity of her emotion—and it reads well. As for exact recounting, well, it is as exact as her memory and her concern for language can make it. Of course, it is in any case a translation from the

French by his translator.

> January 8, 1923
> "I didn't think I would lose you that way. I thought that perhaps you
> would take up with another boy or that perhaps you would get con-
> verted."
> He smiled. "Get converted . . . to what?"
> And then to console me: "But why should you lose me? Why should my
> affection for you change? It isn't the kind of affection that changes.
> *Because it is without passion, without ardor, without enthusiasm, without*
> *flame.*"

Poor Dorothy, receiving this blow:

> And all my happiness of the last three months turned to dust and
> ashes. And he was angry because I showed that it hurt. He has been
> angry with me all the time. He is unjustly angry with me. Angry when
> I don't believe in his love—angrier still when I do.
>
> He took away my papers with him. I knew it would be the end.
> He wrote to me from Rapallo:
> "Why do you refuse constantly to understand that I find it almost
> unbearable to grant . . . even to you—almost anything that could make
> her jealous? Oh! I know, I know, what you can be thinking, but it's
> wrong. For everything else, no matter how important it might be,
> that's what I never could give her. But what you are asking of me is pre-
> cisely what I have vowed to her and save for her. But never, never
> except with Elizabeth—or you—have I felt how deep, jealous, reli-
> gious is my love for her. The cruel thing is that it should be you, pre-
> cisely, who has to know it and suffer from it—and not she."

How can he not see his own cruelty? But it is true that they are both
playing out the charade:

> I burnt what I had written about Pontigny—about our two evenings in
> Paris, about our afternoon in the Luxembourg. He has obliterated all
> that—denied it—effaced it—forgotten it—literally forgotten it,
> I expect. Was it merely pity then. . .
> Does he hate me because of what I wrote and showed him? should
> I have written it differently? Then I should have had to *be* different.
> I know. I know. my insufficiency of intelligence, of heart, of character.
> But how could I hide that from him? I don't want to hide it.
> "How can he always refuse to understand that it was just because
> I never forgot "how deep, jealous, religious" was his love for *her*, that
> I could not understand the necessity, the meaning of his treatment of
> me. I did not think I was asking for "what he vowed to her and saved
> for her." I thought *that* was as impossible as his physical possession—and

therefore why should he grudge me so much less— so infinitely less than he gives to Marc and Elisabeth—to Madame Theo even—to Mme Mayerisch. He never grudges them his presence—his mere presence.

The proofs of his affection for me have been bitter indeed—his confidences—his refusals. But they are proofs—I see it now—whose very cruelty makes them confident. To whom else has he felt it necessary to be cruel?

I think I have been the greatest temptation of his life and the only one he has ever resisted- the only one *worth* resisting (because of its greatness.) [*words crossed through*]

Her over-reading of his feeling is clear—to everyone better, of course.

I used to think he sacrificed me to his wife, because of my little importance—but it is the contrary that is true—there was no *need* for him to sacrifice the others.

"*Greedy*" he said. He has wanted to taste *all* the joys of life & keep besides an inviolate fidelity. Impossible. *I* at any rate can not be crowded into the overflowing measure. He must renounce *me*. I am glad.

He sometimes says he is sorry he didn't stop it—he ought to have stopped it at the beginning—for my sake of course.

He might have very easily—but not without *humiliating* me.

I am grateful to him for never having humiliated me. And now I am safe. However much he hurts me he cannot now touch my pride. [four lines crossed through]

This was the highly charged page to which Gide reacted, in the clinic in Nice, when Martin du Gard brought him her notebook.

Her recounting of the scenes brings it all to painful life. It would be a hard-hearted reader, who would not feel for her, just as if Gide would not feel the scene between Cordelia and Lear:

[no date]

And he answered viciously "Yes, finished! It's all finished." So I got up at once and went away. But later when we were in the drawing room together and he was reading I couldn't bear it any more and I whispered to him "Be kind!" He went on reading but he smiled. And then I screwed up my courage to begin talking to him about Marc. He couldn't resist. In a minute he was friendly again—touched—and amused by my effort and in reality *pleased* as he always is, to talk about him. And from that time till the end every moment I had with him was joy—or better.

During this visit he has been kind to me—more than kind. I have felt his tenderness. I have felt that I touched him. I have felt in him—sometimes—the spontaneity, the élan of a real affection.

In his letters I *never* feel this. (Yes, I have once—twice—in two little sentences.) He is terribly afraid of compromising himself—and me. His feeling is *never* stronger than that fear. Except upon those two occasions he has never *answered* a letter of mine. "Answer! How can I *answer?*" he said to me once, scornfully. (Awful!) He hardly ever, when he writes back, makes even the most distant allusion to anything that I have said. He is as deaf and immovable as a stone (the old comparison of unhappy lovers is really the one I *must* use). How can he—how can he—never, never have an impulse of charity, of anything towards me? And how can I go on writing as I do? It is because in spite of all, I *feel* that he likes it, that he *wants* it. Ah! ah! ah! he *wants* it.

To be sure it is hard to know what Gide "*wants,*" but probably less verbiage.

On his last day after lunch when we were alone in the drawing room I asked him if he was going to "naper." "No, to-day it's no use. Are you?" "No, to-day it's a waste of time." And he repeated "Yes, waste of time." Then he began looking up trains and doing accounts, and sighed "On the eve of a departure I am good for nothing." So I thought that means no more hope for me. Then someone came into the room. He took up his volume of Wordsworth and began to read, and I lay back in the rocking chair opposite to him and shut my eyes in a kind of half dream, opening them from time to time to see whether he was still there. He read for ten minutes after we had been left alone again and then shut the book with another sigh. "Did you sleep?" he asked. "Half and half. I wasn't very far away." He smiled. And then I said "I'm not sorry you are leaving." He got up and went to the window and looked out. "Yes, it is time for me to leave." Then a minute or two afterwards as we were both standing leaning against the mantelpiece, I repeated "I'm not sorry you are leaving." "That's the second time you've said that. Why do you say it? Haven't I been good, kind with you?" "Oh! no, it isn't that. It's that you have left me so much richness that I need time now to count it." "And do you think I am taking nothing from Roquebrune?" And then I said "Will you answer me a question?" He nodded. "Have I ever made your heart beat?" He smiled. "I knew you were going to ask that." Then there was a long pause—a horrid sickening pause for me. "There's a question that words cannot answer. Words are of no use here," he said at last, slowly & gravely. And I stammered out "It's that I can't imagine . . ." and stopped. I meant I can't imagine how it is possible that with my heart beating so there should be no stir in his . . . and yet it would be more difficult to believe that there was. I put my head down between my hands and thought to myself: "I am answered now. Nothing. Nothing. It means there is nothing." Then came the wave of comfort welling up from my heart. It doesn't matter. All I want is to love *him*, and I lifted my head and said "I don't mind really." "Give me your hand." And he was laughing as he took it, laughing with a kind of confident happiness as he kissed it.

Like Dorothy, we begin to feel fateful for any such warm gesture, modest though it be.

> After tea I went and sat on the stone bench (I took good care to take cushions with me!) and waited to him to come back from the village. I heard him laughing again as he came down the steps behind me. Had he seen me? I suppose so but I thought he had Zoum or someone with him. But no! he was alone. He sat down beside me and pulled out the little volume of Shakespeare's Sonnets. "Here's a gift for which you are responsible. Do you think that is so little?" I said he would certainly have discovered them sooner or later without me. "Perhaps," he answered, "but I am glad to owe them to you." "Indeed," I said, "you have every reason to be grateful. It was indeed kind of me." He understood—began to speak—stopped. "It is a strange thing to say perhaps," he said at last, " but it is not of myself I think as I read them, but of you. I read them in communion with you."
>
> And then we read one or two of them together out of the same book and I leant against him, let myself lean against him, oh! so little, and once I put my hand for a second on his hand which was holding the book.

Just as in the Luxembourg Gardens, he had requested her to correct his pronunciation of Keats's "Nightingale." A diversionary tactic, and efficacious. Except that he had read more into his reading than she had. He writes: "I had hoped that in our conversation in the Luxembourg gardens the day I recited the nightingales to you, part of what I said allowed you to understand the meaning behind my silence in regard to you. Reading to you, I made all sorts of reflections." (February 6, 1923, *Letters*, 100) She reflected often also. Often, she felt her age, wishing—oh, how she was wishing—that she were younger and more beautiful. But of course, even then it clearly would not have worked.

> March 27 (1923)
> That evening after dinner I took him into the dining room to write his name in the two books he had given me. *Si le grain ne meurt* and *Corydon*. We sat down at the table and talked in whispers. He told me that S[imon] had been very kind & very "sage" in all he had said, had

given him excellent reasons for not publishing them, at any rate for not publishing them openly. "I know perfectly well," he said, "that if I do it, I am a man adrift on the sea. . . . and still somehow it tempts me."

Then he said "Don't say you won't write me any longer. That would hurt me. And it would disturb me greatly." He said the words quietly and I hesitated, not answering. Then he looked at me—the only time he has ever looked into my eyes. It was the most terrifying moment of my life. His eyes held me, tenderly at first and agreeably. Then they changed. I have never seen such an expression in any eyes. What was it looked from them? something wild and burning. Hunger of the soul—exaltation—well—let me say the word—the thing was there—passion, passion, a kind of agony of passion. I couldn't bear that look for long—it was too terrible and too beautiful. I can only remember desperately flinging my face down upon his hand.

In what kind of a dream have I been living since?

....[her lines of dots]

   Don't let me forget. Don't let me forget. Let me remember that moment when selfishness and vanity are poisoning my heart.
What was his look like that evening? The look of a man already at sea. Passion was in his eyes—a frenzied passion. For me? Oh no-no. Not for me—not that. for everything that he had *missed* in life. the love that he has never known—the love of men and women—a mutual—an equal love. [in pencil, then she redid it in ink and crossed out the next lines]
To think that thousands of people die without ever seeing a look like that.
To think that if I had died as I wanted to four years ago I should have died without seeing his look.

This is a high point of her emotion.
But then, two years later, she reflected back on that time of intensity, comparing what she now had of Gide, far less at ease with her, writing his letters, and having

no time for friendship—no wish for intimacy. There were no talks, no walks . . . I begged him once or twice. I even wept! He pretended not to understand. I thought on the last evening he would give me half an hour and let me—what? sit beside him for a moment or two alone—hold his hand perhaps— hear his voice grow soft. But no—he went away for ever most likely—without a word- a sign.

...

Ah! my dear after all, it is your passionless ardourless friendship that
you promised me was going to be so stable—it is *that* that has changed
before the fantastic wreaths of my imagination.
If you were to read what I have written above when I got your letters I
don't think you would understand any more.
When you renounce, you do it really, once for all. That is true renunciation—to forget what it was that one renounced.
....[lined dots she drew]
Ungrateful that I am. In spite of everything- in spite of reason—in
spite of the evidence of my senses. I *know* that he has not changed.
That all—all—all that has ever been in his heart for me & what has
there not been? is still there.

So then it is better, she writes on November 30, 1927, to let it be.
Were they to be in the same room, he wouldn't feel like speaking, she
wouldn't be able to, he would be saying he was sleepy or cold or nervous, and it would be unpleasant. So much better in writing, therefore, so unfrightening, unlike their face-to-face conversations. So
free. "If I choose I may do the most audacious things. Take your hand
for instance in both of mine and put my cheek upon it and perhaps
my lips." Exactly what Olivia does in Dorothy's novel *Olivia*.

The next year, she saw Gide in Paris, and he apologized, in a fateful
and never-to-be-forgotten letter of March 30, 1928, saying she always
listened too closely, so he would always say stupid things, unlike his
normal self. These are the terrible words:

> when I sense that you expect feelings from me that I am incapable of
> providing and you seem somewhat to disdain those that come natu-
> rally to me—so that with you sometimes it's as though I were in a
> country where the money I have has no currency. I have always to
> "change" it, even if it means losing in the exchange. And even the ges-
> tures you would like *force* me into a short translation full of misinter-
> pretations, for those which seem to you the tenderest are ones I
> instinctively draw back from, which my innermost being refuses to
> assent to. (*Letters*, 119)

This honest and dreadful statement never ceases to have repercus-
sions: in a letter found among her papers, but which Dorothy did not
send, there is a reaction of utmost pain, completely understandable,
surely, whether or not we accept its premise. How, she asks, could she
have possibly given him a friendship less obtrusive? She could not,
she says, have come to him

with fewer expectations, have made fewer claims, fewer advances or even fewer acceptances. The truth is that it is the very fact of your affection for me that makes my presence in your life intolerable to you. You will never lie easily in that premature grave of yours till you have destroyed every trace of tenderness in your heart & mine. (*Letters*, 120)

But that letter was never sent, just preserved. Interesting that she did *not* burn it, as she had some of her own writings she found too harsh. Instead, she sent him another, the next day, about their friendship, and then a few days later, another, about her pain at his letter which had seemed so full of hate.

It had seemed unfair, she said, because this time, when he had put his arm around her, and she had rested her head on his shoulder, she had only felt it "peaceful & pleasant.... There is no rapture—no excitement—no longing. Old age! I suppose so." She had exhausted her grief: "Don't accuse me any more of wishing for what you cannot give. I *don't.* I never disguised it from you when I did. So now you may believe me!" (*Letters*, 121–122)

This terrible letter affair lasted well beyond 1928. On October 1, 1930, at two A.M., Dorothy wrote, daringly, about a visit Gide had just paid Roquebrune:

Dear and beloved, it is so sweet for me to think that I know you so well and so secretly. Nobody could possibly imagine our incongruous friendship ... Did you notice I kissed the lapel of your coat? It was a greater pleasure to me—oh much—than kissing your face: And I dare-say that in reality that's a symbol of my whole attitude.... I believe, I believe, oh, with a transport of joy that you *like* me to love you. (*Letters*, 134)

And then a postscript: "Shall I dare send this?" She did, but then repented, per usual. Later, on the same day: "How can I help being afraid of making you feel uncomfortable, or irritating or offending you in a hundred different ways?" (His letter about currency had clearly showed her this, and, she reiterates, she knows that what he wants is "the desert.") But all the same, she has come to believe that her love "is in some kind of strange way important to you." And Gide takes it lightly, as if in non-reply, responding on October 3, 1930: "you have written me a frightful letter ... but how grateful I am to you for writing me thus." He was not surprised, because he thought as much but (and this is the mortifying part) he knew that he would:

receive a second letter from you, chasing after the first, that tried to undo its effect a little. It came. And I made an immense effort to keep from laughing—a bit the way in certain countries, to applaud they hiss instead of clap their hands. . . . And what I have just said explains why, sometimes, I felt ill at ease in your company." (*Letters*, 133–5)

"As if nothing were amiss," he says, he embraces her. But something is–, or he wouldn't say so, again to her embarrassment. He has certainly not understood her tone, and worse still, has mocked her states of emotion and habitual repentance; so the episode won't really be fixed. On the contrary, it explodes.

In Volume XV of Gide's works, published in the spring of 1939, there is a page of his 1928 *Journal* for March 30, simply substituting for the initials D.B., two that rhyme with them, too close for comfort. Here is the passage, again about the fearful letter the memory of which will yet again destroy Dorothy's confidence, in Gide and, by extension, in herself.

> T.V. would like love; I can only give her friendship. Great as this feeling is, the expectation I sense in her of a more affectionate state falsifies my actions and leads me to the brink of insincerity. I explain this tonight in a letter that will perhaps cause her pain and which it pains me to write. But the fear of causing pain is a form of cowardice which my whole being rebels against.

We have already read him on the subject of causing pain, as his memoirs were bound to do—he was brave, he had implied, not to worry about others, a hurt which he often caused. Dorothy, naturally, reacted to this passage, as it had been published. She writes, on May 3, 1939: "I am terribly afraid you have done something irreparable . . . to my feeling for you. I am very unhappy." Unlike him, she prefers not to cause pain in others, and so has not sent the many other accusatory letters she has written. At first, he doesn't get the reference, then says he wouldn't have written that passage today, in fact, that he had forgotten writing it. And Dorothy: "Is it possible to stab your friend in the heart and then *forget* you have done it?" (*Letters*, 189)

He had in fact already shown her the entry before it was printed, and when, on that occasion, she had sobbed, in hurt and ultimate embarrassment, he had declared he would keep it private. Now he had published it, forgetting his promise. "I feel humiliated," she said.

Worse still, this passage now was to serve as a perfect alibi for Gide, she says, preserving his reputation for fidelity at her expense. Was it perhaps carelessness? Could he please make her believe that at least? Yes, he replies, "I may have been cruel sometimes." But, for him, the only feeling that ever counted was the present one.

He reiterates, how he greatly dislikes chasing after her letters. (*Letters*, 188–194) He will continually remain elusive, *insaissable*, "Gidian" as she says.

Yet of years later, he will maintain he cannot do without her letters, underlining that statement by pointing out that he now always carries with him, like a talisman, a quite extraordinary letter she wrote on April 29, 1942:

> Wednesday evening
> My very Dear, I who have written you so many love letters, thought I should never be able to write you one again, but here I am once more after so long an absence. I thought the only kind thing I could do for you was to keep away, to pretend indifference, to *achieve* indifference, since that I thought was what you wanted. It is only so that I can serve him, I thought. He shall not suffer pity or remorse for me. I will kill my love since it is a nuisance to him. And sometimes I thought I was very near succeeding. But I can't think any of that any more tonight. The sweetness came back, to your voice and your eyes—sweeter, ah, than they have ever been before. But it is not happiness you can give me, not happiness that I want from you, something deeper, fiercer, more like anguish. It has to be bought—perhaps with anguish—I know, I know, it can only come very rarely.
> > . . .
> > This morning you were very near me, your cheek on mine, your lips so near to mine. But no I did not dare. That must be reserved for dreams. They have sometimes come.
> Good-night , my very dear.
> Tear this into a thousand pieces & drop them in the sea.
> Yr D. (*Letters*, 209 -210)

And still years later, on August 16, 1945, in a letter signed "Very tenderly," he says he is still carrying around that letter of hers that he knows by heart, and could not bear to have dropped into the sea or anywhere else. (*Letters*, 245)

There is a postscript to this story, about *Olivia by Olivia*. Like the more recent *Story of O*, this anonymously published story of O has a fascinating tale to it and its provenance.

In 1949, Dorothy Bussy published, anonymously, a brief tale—subsequently to acquire a certain fame—called *Olivia*. It is dedicated to V.W., clearly Virginia Woolf, whose Hogarth Press published it, with the requested anonymity. Dorothy had shown it to Gide fourteen years earlier, in 1933, unsure whether she would ever show it to the world, but sure she must show it to him. ("For whether you will or no you have to bear a part in all I think and feel and do." Even the P.S. in which she announces this "*deadly*" secret, twice underlined she commented on." "Oh! these postscripts. How dangerous!"). She mailed it to him on December 30, 1933, "disgusted with it—poor, meagre, inadequate thing." (*Letters*, 153–4) She feared sending it to him, "of all people in the world," perhaps as an indecent gesture of saying too much yet again.

Olivia takes place at "Les Avons," in an agreable forest near Paris: Les Avons is modeled on Marie Souvestre's "Les Ruches", in Fontainebleau, a girl's school attended by two Bussy daughters. The heroine is instantly attracted by the face of "Laura," the favorite of Mlle Julie, and therefore detested by Julie's devoted assistant Mlle Cara, as someone points out to Olivia. Then, fatally, the flame of Olivia's passion for Mlle Julie is lit by Mlle Julie's reading aloud of Racine. (Given the preponderant place in the lives, and letters, of Dorothy and Gide, of reading aloud, the passage awakens us instantly, as it did Olivia, to "the breaking down of barriers" occasioned by that act. There are a surprising number of photographs of Gide reading aloud at Pontigny, surrounded by listeners.)

The description here of the awakening of Olivia's love for Mademoiselle Julie reflects the situation we have seen all too well. No wonder, perhaps, that Gide did not originally read to himself accurately this little tale about reading aloud:

> The listener is suddenly given the freedom of a city at whose gates he would never have dreamt of knocking. He may enter forbidden precincts.
> He may communicate at the most sacred altars with a soul he has never dared, never will dare, approach, watch without fear or shame a spirit that has dropped its arms, its veils, its prudences, its reserves. He who is not beloved may gaze and hearken and learn at last what nothing else will ever reveal to him and what he longs to know even at the cost of life itself—how the beloved face is moved by passion, how scorn sits upon those features and anger and love. How the beloved's voice softens and trembles into tenderness or breaks in the anguish of jealousy and grief . . . (Olivia, 31)

The clue to the situation is given by the phrase "he who is not beloved." The story is all the more interesting for it being, as with Dorothy, a flame ignited in an English mind and heart by a French voice—Dorothy Bussy the translator/writer, writing here in English, has here a double attraction to the flame of the Other: his voice, his language, her ability to make his language into her language . . . the elements are there. For a great tragedy, Racinian, or simply a great tale of love.

Gide did not get the point. He read "with a keen emotion those pathetic reminiscences . . ." (!) And heard her voice through that flame and then forgot it. How could I have been so idiotic? mused Dorothy in 1948, as to send it to him—and in parentheses she added ("We don't want women who write in our cities!") For she had now shown the book to Rosamund Lehman, and John Lehman, and Leonard Woolf ("A man, I thought, he won't like it & I shall be saved any more trouble") and it would be coming out in the fall: "So now, dear friend, perhaps you will have the glory of having rejected two best sellers—Proust and yours truly! But you won't write me such a nice letter as you wrote him." (*Letters*, 277–8)

But Gide, who now perhaps got the point of *Olivia*, did send her a telegram, saying simply, "As repentant and embarrassed as with Proust," and then a letter saying how he had devoured it, "hungrily, delightedly, with anguish, intoxication . . . it all came to life anew, . . . palpitating life, suffering flesh, poetry and reality at once." He now could admire its restraint and reserve, modesty and candor, and marveled at the scales that must have covered his eyes on first reading. (We marvel also.) And Dorothy replied how glad she was, for of course what she had wanted him to recognize was that *Olivia* had only been possible because of his presence, teaching, and example, in her life. "I am glad that Olivia after so many years of patience, has at last succeeded in touching you, as she would have wished." (*Letters*, 283–4)

I don't read the tale of Dorothy and Gide as a tragedy or a parody of infatuation, mimicking some more proper love, whether hetero or homosexual. It has, I think, its own dignity. What it most surely has is its own passion about reading, writing, and translating.

When she was seventy-nine, in 1944, feeling herself "growing very old," with her hair and teeth falling out, with her eyes, ears, and memory failing, walking with a stick, Dorothy was still excited, as was

Gide, about their reading, and their correspondence about it. She was still always reading: Oscar Wilde and Graham Greene and Cyril Connolly, and feeling close to E.M. Forster, who had been the center of the Bloomsbury group since the death of Roger Fry. On the other hand, she was absorbed by Cicero's letters to Atticus (which she read in Latin), and was often quoting, in her letters to Gide, Virgil and Shakespeare and Marvell and Keats. Gide was also always reading: Walter Pater and Jane Austen, and D.H. Lawrence (whom, at one point, he confuses with T.E. Lawrence, as Dorothy pointed out) and Charles Lamb, as Dorothy recommended. Gide was reading his friend Paul Valéry, disliking his later writings in their "mannered mode," and was then, as he expressed it to Dorothy, mournful at his death. They sorrowed together at the death of Proust on November 18, 1922. They shared, always, so much.

To return, finally, to the poetry of Cordelia's meeting with Lear: cited by Dorothy with such passion, it seems to me that this tale of Dorothy Bussy and André Gide has its own poetry, and its own restraint, as do *Olivia* and her author. Dorothy had translated her love into this story. "I must feed on beauty and rapture in order to grow strong," says Olivia. (34) And it was fine that the love of Olivia, like that of Dorothy, was greater than that of the beloved: fine and acceptable that she was the one to cover the beloved's hand with kisses, sobbing: "It was I alone who loved—it was I alone whose love was an impossible fantasy." (Olivia, 83)

But here's the great part. When Roger Martin du Gard had made a very clumsy translation of *Olivia* in 1948, from Dorothy's rough sketch in French—for he knew next to no English—Gide complained of the translation, and right after, said, in three famous words of English that he and Dorothy understood perfectly, "*I love you.*" Dorothy was eighty-three. She replied, in a modest postscript: "I do believe those three English words in your letter. I believe, you know, you understand, you mean them." They had understood from the beginning, as sensitive translators, what it all meant.

It seems to me, in this way that life and work and emotion have finally merged, that the placement of this essential and essentially true expression is infinitely indicative of the depth and power of translation, since it occurs exactly after Gide's commentary on what he sees, in a bad translation of *Olivia*, as a betrayal of the most intimate possession one has: one's writing. Dorothy, the loving translator, had never betrayed him.

At the end, nine years after Gide's death, Dorothy's mind grew foggy. Simon had died long before, and their daughter Janie had died in an electrical accident two weeks before; Dorothy was, happily, unaware of this. She peacefully passed away, in 1960, at age ninety-five. In the long run, Gide did not betray her, either. On January 9, 1951, a few weeks before his death, he exclaimed: "I need to write to you, without however having anything to say." For that kind of need speaks more triumphantly than whatever words might be uttered.

Chapter 4

Emily Carr

Setting Out in the Forest

You'll never quite catch up. There will always be a beyond. It would be terrible to catch up—the end of everything. Oh God, let me never catch up till I die. Let me be always feeling up and out, beyond and beyond into eternity.

—*Emily Carr, Hundreds and Thousands*

See now "the funny fat lady with the monkey and the wheelchair." (Blanchard, 224) Emily Carr was never like anyone else, neither in her being nor in her painting. Her colors were strong, as were her sweeping lines—she preferred the native customs and art, and the wild expanses of forest and sea, to anything domestic or personal: she did not, said all her critics and admirers, paint like a female. Of course not, she would have said. "This one should have been a boy," her father would have said.

Compared frequently to Georgia O'Keeffe, Emily Carr stood out among artists and among people, not just by her creations, in painting and writing, but by her appearance and lifestyle. She was well-known as Victoria's "oddity," Emily in her shapeless smocks, her hairnet and velvet headband, her men's boots cut down to size and her old felt hat and coat, her irritable personality, and her band of animals, among which the star was the Capuchin monkey called Woo, always attached to her waist by a small chain. Woo was dressed in little pinafores, doll-sized, of which she would tear off the hooks and buttons, until finally Emily used buckles. Woo was mischievous beyond anyone else's being able to stand it: she would smash her drinking cup through the window, tear the tiles off the roof, pull up the floorboards to find whatever she could digest, and generally misbehave. At the end of Emily's life, Woo was given to the Stanley Park Zoo.

Emily, preferring animals to people, had many other animals, to name only a few among them:

> The Cockatoo Sallie
> The two Old English Bobtails, she called the Bobbies
> Other dogs: David, Adam, Moses, Noah
> The cats Twinkie and Dolf, and other cats
> The parrots Rebecca and Josephine and Hamby, and some others
> A chipmunk
> Several budgerigars
> The Belgian gryphons Koko and Ginger Pop and Tantrum
> And, the white rat Susie, so loving that she would scurry up the stairs each night to crawl across Emily's pillow: when Susie died, her little nose was found pointing at the stairs, ready to go. . . .

At one point in her journal, she exclaims, in despair over having no friends of her own age: "Oh God, why did you make me a pelican and sit me down in a wilderness? . . . Oh Lord, I thank Thee for the dogs and the monkey and the rat." (Complete Works, 757)

Now, Emily Carr's commentators are fortunate, in that she loved writing, both journals and letters. As she said of herself, "there is a side of friendship that develops better and stronger by correspondence than contact, especially with some people who can get their thoughts clearer when they see them written." (Shadbolt, 12)

She didn't start out particularly odd, was in fact the bestlooking of her family's five sisters, although she was "contrary from the start." Even at her baptism, she manifested her temper: "Dr. Reid hung on to a curl and a button long enough to splash water on my hair ribbon and tell God I was Emily; then the button burst off and I wrenched the curl from his hand. . . ." (*Growing*, 3) The priest was surprised, like the surgeon delivering Judith Gautier at her birth, whose hand she bit. "Who is this monster," the priest asked?

The sisters, although Emily's depreciation of them in relation to her art is vivid, ended up, in later life, living rather close together, sharing meals sometimes. Alice and Emily traveled together (to Alaska in 1907, to see native carvings; to England, in 1900–1905, for Emily to study; and to France in 1910–1911, for Emily to experience French painting). They needed each other, for neither had ever married. Emily—Milly to the family—had had someone in love with her: Mayo Paddon, who had even followed her to France to propose marriage. But art came first, and she had been violently put off anything sexual by what she termed her father's "brutal telling" her about such things early on. She never forgot. Her adored mother died when she was fourteen (she makes it twelve in her own writing: " I was twelve when Mother died—the raw, green Victoria age, twelve years old") (*Growing*, 4) and her very "ultra English" father died when she was sixteen. "I loved mother best." (Shadbolt, 21)

All the same, she paints an intoxicating picture of her father

> hurrying to tend Isabella, the great, purple-fruited grapevine that crawled half over our house and entirely over Father's heart. Her grapes were most beautifully fogged with dusky bloom, behind which she pretended her fruit was luscious; but they were really tough-skinned, sour old grapes.
> Father was burstingly proud of miserable old Isabella. (*Growing*, 5)

How wonderful that he should be "bursting" like the grapes, fogged over as concerns his children, perhaps, but at least in love with something.

A most engaging description of a picnic with her mother gives a picture of everything Proustianly possible in childhood: the delights of a special time and a special smell, taste, and privilege, because she has given to the daughter "a whole afternoon of herself."

> It was wild lily time. We went through our garden, our cow-yard and pasture, and came to our wild lily field. Here we stood a little, quietly looking. Millions upon millions of white lilies were spangled over the green field. Every lily's brown eye looked down into the earth but her petals rolled back over her head and pointed at the pinetree tops and the sky. The perfume was delicate yet had such power its memory clung through the rest of your life and could carry you back any time to the old lily field, even after the field had become city and there were no more lilies in it—just houses and houses. Yes, even then your nose could ride on the smell and come galloping back to the lily field.
>   While the child made a daisy chain, the mother sewed, beneath the great spiraea bushes "loaded with droops of creamy blossom having a hot, fluffy smell. In these, bees droned and butterflies fluttered, but our mock-orange bush was whiter and smelled stronger and sweeter." (*Growing*, 8)

The joy of this scene and others goes a long way toward explaining why she was always, to herself, "Small."

The smells and sights are from the beginning memorable, like the cow smell in the cowyard that "cosied up things," to offset the other odors. Her intense descriptions are among the captivating elements of Emily's writings—begun early, but not really taken up as a career until she was almost seventy, in 1937—so that all her bestknown writings date between that date and 1941. Very often the "facts," the characters, and certainly the dates, as given in the writings do not correspond to her life. Fiction took over frequently, as it tends to in autobiographies: for example, she ascribes the famous "brutal telling" administered by her father to "Mrs. Piddington," in San Francisco. In the journals as tidied up and published with success by Ira Dilworth, who had taken them to Oxford University Press in 1940, disagreeable descriptions of people and other things of like nature are removed. Her angry disposition, her feeling when very young that she should have been a boy, her continual supposing that her work was undervalued, her detestation of "the critics"—and, in general, her longing to thumb her nose at polite society—all this comes over clearly, even as it is presumably tempered by the editor.

One of her stories, in the *Book of Small*, perfectly illustrates the kind of anger she had against those who wouldn't see or listen or pay attention to anything outside themselves. It has exactly the same feeling as her diatribes, published and not, on the subject of "critics"—how they don't see. Showing her distrust and dislike of organized religion, it also illustrates by extension her great dislike of institutions in general (including the Island Arts and Crafts, the Vancouver Ladies' Art Club, and so on). Here, she looks back at herself, "Small," and her first pet, which, we note in the opening sentence, she has earned, so that it is more than simply a gift. The story goes deep. It is simply called "The Bishop and the Canary."

> Small had earned the canary and loved him . . .
> . . .
> Her lovely bird! Because there was no one else to show him to she must show him to the Bishop. Birds belonged to the sky. The Bishop would understand.
> "Look, Bishop! Look at my bird!
> She stood before him with the cage held high. "Bishop! Oh please Bishop, see!"
> Dimly the Bishop became aware of some object obstructing his way.
> He laid a dimpled hand upon the little girl's head. "Ah, child," he said, "you are a pretty picture." And moved her gently from his path.
> The Bishop went his way. The child stood still.

"My beautiful bird!"
The look of hurt fury which she hurled at the Bishop's back might
have singed his clerical broadcloth. (24–5)

For Emily, institutions were part of the big sham of the universe.
Her lifelong campaign was directed against "sham." . . . "She found it
everywhere, in English manners, formal religion, art critics,
philistines, rival artists, and suspiciously often in the close relations
of her friends." In their arguments, which can become quite heated,
"things are flung, hurled, slammed, scrubbed, snapped, smacked,
seized and pushed." (*Growing*, 11)
She had always wanted to be an artist, scratching portraits on paper
bags, making for herself an easel out of cherry sticks. At sixteen, she
pleaded to go to art school in San Francisco, and then in 1900, to
London, to the Westminster School, where the hyper-Bloomsbury
Duncan Grant would study in 1902. She spent five years in England,
until 1905, and painted in many places: from St. Ives in picturesque
Cornwall to Bushey in Hertfordshire, which had been recommended to
her. Her tales are colorful to say the least.
Her studies with Julius Olsson in St. Ives did not go well. He was a
celebrated painter of seascapes and clearly wished his students to
emulate him. And he also insisted that painters stand at their easels.
Emily had had a toe infection, following which the toe had to be
amputated, and as a consequence she could neither stand for a long
time nor walk for long distances. When she painted, she had to use
the campstool she always carried.

Ohlsson exclaimed
"Sitting to work!"
"Bad foot, sir."
"Huh! I did say the sands, didn't I? Sunshine on sea and white boats."
"If you please, sir, the glare of sea and white sand blind me with
headache."
"Neurotic! Morbid!" Olsson would yell . . .

Fortunately, he alternated lessons with Algernon Talmage, who
helped her do just what she wanted, painting in Treganna Woods
above St. Ives. "And there was John Whiteley . . . were saluted by
Emily later, in *Growing Pains*: 'Bless John Whitely! Bless Algernon
Talmage! The two painting masters who first pointed out to
me . . . that there was coming and going among trees, that there was
sunlight in shadows.' (261)"

But over and over, she was not well physically. After her toe was amputated in 1900, in London, she repeatedly had breakdowns — some ascribed by various commentators to sexual repression, some to just plain physical ailments. At one point, she was placed in a sanatorium, mostly inhabited by tuberculosis victims — about this she wrote a book called *Pause*, in which she describes the "electricity" used on her. This was perhaps an exaggeration, since electric shock did not exist at this point, and it was most probably the sort of wand used by chiropractors even now. She was perhaps anemic, and certainly had a limp from her amputated toe. In later life, she had back trouble, to such an extent that she could no longer carry her palette on her back to the woods where she loved to paint. This is at the origin, in fact, of her taking up writing — when she could no longer undertake her painting trips. All of this being true, it does seem remarkable that she was able to do so very much.

Back in Victoria, she had nothing but loathing for the desperately colonial old-world Royalist Empress hotel. There, she hated "all the 'pink teas' and the supreme dowdiness of the teadrinkers: their horrible clothes, horrible manners, horrible looks . . . Dumpy little women sitting in outsized stuffed chairs, feet dangling and turned in, frightful hats, geranium gashes for mouths, acting up, not one bit themselves, simpering at men, overacting. . . ." (Blanchard, 265)

In 1906, she moved to Vancouver to a boarding house at 541 Burrard street, and had a studio at 570 Granville, where she painted and showed her art. These seemed to be the happy years: her studio was always thronged with visitors. A Salish woman named Sophie Frank, who sold baskets, became her great friend; when she died, years later, Emily felt the loss as a terrible one.

Always she had explored the northern wilds of the Canadian coast, plunging into her encounters with First Nation art and villages, meeting many of the various tribes. She traveled to Alert Bay, Campbell River, and other Kwakiutl villages. Her ability to render the intricacies of totem poles far outreached that of any other painter. Her reflections on the painting of these poles and on the mind of the carvers who created them tells us an immense amount about both her way of creating and why the observer feels so unusually drawn *into* her renderings of poles and towering trees. Just as each woods or forest is for her a portrait of the relations between the trees, so each pole has its own conversation between the figures, in their "strong talk":

The Indian totem pole is not easy to draw. . . . The Indian used distortion, sometimes to fill spaces but mostly for more powerful expressing

than would have been possible had he depicted actualities—gaining
strength, weight, power by accentuation. . . . Totems were less valued
for their workmanship than for their "talk."
Indian art broadened my seeing, loosened the formal tightness I had
learned in England's schools. Its bigness and stark reality baffled my
white man's understanding. . . . I had been schooled to see outsides
only, not struggle to pierce.
The Indian caught first at the inner intensity of his subject, worked
outward to the surfaces. (*Growing*, 211–12)

Her own paintings of forests, as well as to terms, work from the
inside out.

In 1908, she became a founding member of the British Columbia
Society of Fine Arts, and exhibited with them for much of her life.

After holding a studio show and putting some work up for auction
to have sufficient funds to travel, Emily left Canada in 1910 with Alice
for a year's study in Paris, and lived on the rue Campagne première,
famously the home of many artists, including the photographer Man
Ray. Emily knew no French, so she worked entirely with English
speakers.

She met the English artist Harry Phelan Gibb, who suggested she
study at the Académie Colarossi, but she preferred to study privately
with John Duncan Fergusson, a Scot. She left his atelier because of
falling sick, and then, after recuperating in Sweden, went with the
Gibbs family to Crécy-en-Brie, and then to northern Brittany, to the
village of St. Efflam. Her paintings from this period seem far less
adventurous than those of her later work, but she hung two of them
in the Salon d'Automne in Paris in 1911.

Of all her painter teachers, only the New Zealander Frances
Hodgkins, whom she met and studied watercolour with in the walled
town of Concarneau, was a woman. The time in France, where she
met few of the artists so excitedly turning out their work in Paris,
does not seem to have left much of a mark on her—of all her canvasses during the Paris years, perhaps only *The Brittany Kitchen*, now
in Montreal, stands out. It hangs proudly with other paintings of
Emily Carr, donated by Max Stern, the collector. It has the same
unmistakable feeling of warmth as the cow smell "cosying up" the
cowyard in Small's childhood, and as her relation to all her animals, to
Johnny the pony when she was indeed small, taking her to "the deep
lovely places that were the very foundation on which my work as a
painter was to be built." (*Growing*, 14) Just as the Indians' totems
taught her to carve and see and think from the inside out to the surfaces, so the strength of her art, in such a domestic space, relatively

rare for her, and in the more familiar larger ones outside, was from the beginning built on an interior knowledge. Sometimes it was conferred by just one smell, like that of the lilies on her picnic so long before, with her adored mother.

Then in 1911 Emily Carr returned home, having not made extensive ventures in France. She certainly ventured in her own region and further afield. A great deal of her time was spent in the great stretches and solitudes of Stanley Park in Vancouver, a forest of towering trees. "Alone, I went there to sketch, loving its still solitudes—no living creature but dog Billie and me. . . ." (*Growing*, 207) But still she traveled to coastal and central northern British Columbia, in the Alert Bay region, the Skeena River valley, and the Haida villages of the Queen Charlotte Islands. Over the years, she would travel extensively, certainly more than any other white painter, in the Gitksan (Tsimshan) villages; in Sitka; and more.

Alas, in Vancouver, in 1912, after her return from France, her paintings did not sell, from her studio at 1465 West Broadway, probably because her art seemed "too advanced." In *Growing Pains*, her autobiography, she called this being rejected, and, having no pupils, and no sales, had to give up her studio in Vancouver and move back to Victoria in 1913. "Nobody bought my pictures. I had no pupils; therefore I could not afford to keep on the studio." (All the art, she said, had been smashed out of her.) So she built an apartment house at 646 Simcoe Street, and became a rental agent, a manager, and a janitor. Later she would write up these discouraging experiences, in her prickly manner, in *The House of All Sorts*.

What did she not try? She raised dogs for sale, Old English Bobtail Sheepdogs and subsequently wrote tales of the Bobtails, sold fruit, and took up pottery at the age of forty, working long hours over the kiln and selling her wares at the Empress Hotel and at a gift shop in Vancouver. She continued the pottery until 1930. It was always a struggle; the kiln was a veritable ordeal:

> Stacking, stoking, watching, testing, I made hundreds and hundreds of stupid objects, the kind that tourists pick up. . . . I hated myself for prostituting Indian art; our Indians did not "pot," their designs were not intended to ornament clay—but I did keep the Indian design pure. Because my stuff sold, other potters followed in my lead and, knowing nothing of Indian Art, falsified it. (*Growing*, 231)

She painted very little during the years 1914–1927, having to earn a living. Over and over, discouragement set in. And she rarely felt supported psychologically by her sisters. Even as the material context was unforgiving ("Victoria had boomed, now she slumped"), there she was painting the sort of thing that was next to taboo: "one sister painted china. Beyond mention of that, Art was taboo in the family. My kind was considered a family disgrace."

To compound the problem, in the outside world, the provincial government turned down her paintings, the cultural institutions of Western Canada ridiculed her "striving for bigness, depth," and she was just plain ahead of her time. "The general attitude was that she was pretty queer and her work was queerer . . . just too powerful for Victoria. This attitude lasted for years and she was roundly criticized in the backwards society that was Victoria." (Blanchard, 147)

However, things were about to brighten, if slowly (in the slowness that was Victoria, and even Vancouver at that period). In 1924, a buyer for the Canadian Pacific Railway gift shops in Banff, Kate Mather, was in Victoria for the winter. She had read a review about the "usual atrocities" a Miss Carr had exhibited with the Island Arts and Crafts Society. Then one day she was apartment hunting, and saw a sign in the house where Emily was renting space on Simcoe Street. She knocked and entered a vestibule filled with native baskets, then a hallway lined with paintings, then a studio. While she was marveling at the art work, suddenly there

> came this person, I should say—that's about all you could call her at that time—dressed in a gunny sack, her hair all tied up with velvet ribbon, her arms akimbo. She just shrieked at me. She said: "How dare you walk into my house like this?" . . . I said, "These pictures—where in the world do they come from?" "Well," she said, "they're mine."
> (Blanchard, 160)

They made friends, and it was to Kate Mather that Emily would go at night to complain of her hard day's work. During the day she had been a hostess and a landlady, and at night she would rage over the indignities of the past hours.

Eventually Emily the painter was befriended and defended by several people in helpful positions: Eric Brown, of the Canadian National Gallery; Marius Barbeau, Government Anthropologist: Max Stern, a collector from Montreal; and others. Both the turning points in her life are clearly marked; the first occurs in 1927, when, at the prompting of Eric Brown, she left the provincialism of Victoria and the bustling new commerce of Vancouver to cross the mountains, through Winnipeg, to the eastern part of Canada, where she met—unforgettably—the painters, all men, of the so-called Group of Seven. Frederick B. Housser had written of them in his book *A Canadian Art Movement*, which she read, at Brown's suggestion, and then encountered them. She longed to meet these explorers, each of whom would, as Housser described it, "suit new materials to new methods . . . one who divests himself of the velvet coat and flowing tie of his caste, puts on the outfit of the bushwhacker and prospector; closes with his environment; paddles, portages, and makes camp; sleeps in the out-of-doors under the stars; climbs mountains with his sketch box on his back." (Blanchard, 173)

These painters had worked above Lake Superior, and those stern mountains "cradling the cloud." They had read Emerson, Thoreau, and her favorite, Whitman. Among the group, she was particularly impressed by the paintings of, and the personality and generosity of Lawren Harris, her great friend for many years after that. Welcoming her, he had made to her the same remark Degas had made to Suzanne Valadon that changed her life: "You are one of us." (Blanchard, 177) Seeing his paintings, she had a kind of epiphany her entire way of seeing, being, and painting were transformed. What she says of her personal emotions, she might have said also of her personal admirations:" I don't love many, but when I do I love *hard*." (*Growing*, 12)

She writes in her journal about this crucial discovery: "Oh, God, what have I seen? Where have I been? Something has spoken to the very soul of me, wonderful, mighty, not of this world. . . . Something has called out of somewhere. Something in me is trying to answer." (Nov. 17, 1927, Journal, 67) But of course, she remains conscious that they are seven men, and she is one woman, and she from the other side of the Rockies—the division between eastern and western Canada still sensible. And so she has been reflecting:

> I wonder if these men feel as I do, that there is a common chord struck between us. No, I don't believe they feel so toward a woman. I'm way behind them in drawing and in composition and rhythm and planes, but I know inside me what they're after and I feel that perhaps, given a chance, I could get it too. Ah, how I have wasted the years! But there are still a few left.
>
> Oh, these men, this Group of Seven, what have they created? A world stripped of earthiness, shorn of fretting details, purged, purified; a naked soul, pure and unashamed; love spaces filled with wonderful serenity. . . . those silence, awe-filled spaces . . . . (Nov. 16–17, 1927, Journals, 6–7)

She feels, under the guidance of Lawren Harris, that the visible universe is "the living body of an inexpressibly beautiful and benevolent spiritual force." And this will motivate her in her own search for the soul of Canada. She, Emily Carr, whose paintings Harris so admired, would do, could do, for the western part of Canada what the entire Group of Seven did for the east. She would, as they did, paint the epic of her land. As the epic poets formerly had celebrated Europe, she would celebrate Canada, its western spaces: her very writing, as her thinking, is Whitmanian.

And she has felt it before meeting them, while crossing the Rockies: she had always believed that "There is something bigger than fact: the underlying spirit, all it stands for, the mood, the vastness, the wildness, the Western breath of go-to-the-devil-if-you-don't-like-it, the eternal big spaceness of it. Oh the West! I'm of it and I love it." As well as welcoming her and inspiring her, Harris shared his methods with her he would rub raw linseed oil on to the canvas and paint over that, and retouch his dark colors. He suggested books to read, including Clive Bell's *Art*, and assured her they would always keep in touch, as they did for many years.

She returned west, knowing it was time to paint the countryside she so loved: "It was my own country, part of the West and me," and she was determined to see the mountains "in a bigger way. . . . How I do want to learn more about space!" (December 5 and 18, 1927, Journals, 12 and 19). So she would set out, over and over, with a sketching pad on her shoulder, and, always, a dog at her heels: "I went into the woods singing . . . household tasks shrivelled as the importance of my paintings swelled." She had already spent a great deal of time exploring, painting First Nation villages and tribes. But Lawren Harris had advised her to do her own work now, and she found him to be right:

"Put aside the Indian motifs, strike out for yourself, Emily, inventing, creating, clothing ideas born of this West, ideas that you feel deep rooted in your heart," I sat before the woods and stared, lost, frustrated. . . . When I had discovered my subject, I sat before it for some while before I touched a brush, feeling my way into it, asking myself these questions, "What attracted you to this particular subject? Why do you want to paint it? What is its core, the thing you are trying to express?" (Journals, 263–5)

Her notebook she always carried was helpful in exactly this manner, for she would "word" a painting before she did it.

She had collected a great many Indian artifacts and had made drawings and paintings of them, then offering them to the provincial government. They were turned down. As the critics mocked her, and she felt rejected, she also found the process of exhibiting her work hateful. Always, she was ill at ease, disquiet, lonely: "I made no new friends; one does not after schooldays unless there are others who are going your way or who have interests in common. Nobody was going my way, and their way did not interest me. I took my sheepdog and rode out to the woods." (*Journals*, 203) As for institutions, she was as against them as she had been in the beginning. The Bishop had represented what organized religion was, and the various clubs represented what organized culture could be.

As an example of her opinion of organizations, she felt strongly about the Island Arts and Crafts Club and "its addled existence. A very select band of elderly persons, very prehistoric in their ideas on Art." And then there was the Vancouver Ladies' Art Club: "a cluster of society women who intermittently packed themselves and their admirers into a small rented studio to drink tea and jabber art jargon." Finally, she said, "that rootless organization . . . withered, died." It was transformed into a Fine Arts Society, at the exhibitions of which "My pictures were hung either on the ceiling or on the floor and jeered at, insulted; members of the 'Fine Arts' joked at my work, laughing with reporters. Press notices were humiliating." (*Growing*, 205)

So, repeatedly, she felt snubbed and rejected by these clubs; marvelously, then, that rejection helped to *starch* her: "My pride stiffened, my energy crisped. I fetched my sheep-dog and cage of bullfinches from Victoria, added a bunch of white rats, a bowl of goldfish, a cockatoo and a parrot to my studio equipment and fell into vigorous, hard, happy work. . . . (*Growing*, 207) Perhaps, then, the difficult times were useful for the backbone: "The storm has never quite lulled in my life." (December 12, 1927, *Journals*, 16)

There was worse. In 1930, she wrote: "I went east this spring . . . found Harris had shown some of my letters to others. That upset me." This desire not to be seen in one's inside, or even on one's outside—not to have to be present at the sight of the *others* gazing at one's paintings, listening to one's lectures, reading one's private words—was intense. Any display necessarily included more than one wanted to reveal. Later, in 1938, during a one-man show at the Vancouver Gallery, she will again dread anyone seeing "my thoughts, my way of seeing," dread the way the artist stands "naked before all those eyes." Terrible times. Her shock over Harris showing her letters is reminiscent for us of Carrington's fervent desire not to have others see her portrait of Lytton, which so clearly announces her adoration of him.

Somewhere else was where she wanted to be, continuing her explorations of Indian missions and Indian houses. "I travelled in anything that floated in water or crawled over land." (Shadbolt, 30) Her final trip to Indian sites on Vancouver Island took place. And always her love of nature was the uppermost element in her journals and her vision, broadened as it was, progressively, not just by her Indian experiences that so freed her from her formalistic phase, but by everything natural of which she felt part and that she anthropomorphized, joyful at doing so: "Oh, these mountains, great bundle of contradiction, hard, cold, austere, disdainful, remote yet gentle, spiritually appealing! Oh, you mountains, I am at your feet . . ." (36, June 17, 1931)

A month later that year there was another turning point, which would greatly influence her travels for four years: she purchased the largest animal she was ever to have—a van called the Elephant, in which she could camp with all her brood. The freedom this permitted her was extreme, and well-earned. First, the van appeared to her like a vision, in July of 1931, as the opposite of beauty: "Sure enough, there she sat, her square ugliness bathed in summer sunshine, and I sang in my heart." (Journals, 45) Here she describes one of her camping trips, with the Elephant, and its domestic alternative, interleaved with nostalgia:

> To sit on a perfectly decent chair with four steady legs on a wood floor, to eat at a solid table with four even legs, to have a plaster ceiling instead of a sky quivering with movement and light, to turn the tap and apply a match instead of adjusting the stove-pipe to meet the wind and collecting sticks from the woods and axing and bucksawing a bit and blinking the smoke out of one's eyes and blacking one's hands (but oh, the lovely smoke smell and taste), to spread out in a wide bed and look over dim house roofs and chimneys (I remember the moon through the pine trees), to have a whole room to oneself instead of sharing a little van with monkey, dogs and rat!. but God's a little closer out there and the earth and sky and trees are very sweet. The house shuts these things out a little. (September 29, 1934, Journals, 150)

And here she is, painting outside, and illustrating the movement that is by now the basis of her work. It is the rhythm that counts, and that pulls the observer into the painting—the swirling lines, approximating the spirit in nature, must be articulated carefully, so as not to jerk the vision, or halt it in its sweep:

> I am painting a sky. A big tree butts up into it on one side, and there is a slope in the corner with pines. These are only to give distance. The subject is sky, starting lavender beneath the trees and rising into a smoother hollow air space, greenish in tone, emerging into laced clouds and then into deep, bottomless blue, not flat and smooth like the centre part of the sky, but loose, coming forward. There is to be *one* sweeping movement through the whole air, an ascending movement, high and fathomless. The movement must connect with each part, taking great care with the articulation. A movement floating up. (February 8, 1935, Journals, 170)

The witness she bears to the forests and dark silent trees and wilderness, to the beaches and skies of the Pacific coast, is tremendous. Its power is unmistakable. She painted the epic of western Canada, as Lawren Harris had known she was to do. In his article "The Paintings and Drawings of Emily Carr," he wrote of her being the first artist to discover this world, of her "love of its moods, mystery and majesty that gave it the quality of indwelling spirit which the Indians knew so well." Living with them, he said, she was empowered in a way that no white person had been before.

And here it was that her religious feeling, more powerful as she grew older, grew apace. She found "soul" in everything, and spent much of her time trying to get her thoughts to stand still long enough to be put down on paper as well as in paint; the trouble is "because everything is always on the move, always expanding." (Shadbolt, 19) She investigated the kind of theosophy that Harris espoused, but finally rejected it for her own individual religious feeling: God in everything, a kind of pantheism that infuses her paintings after 1930. In a box where she kept her favorite poems, she kept poems by Edna St. Vincent Millay and by Sara Teasdale about the presence of God in the world, His world. The exact other pole from her young experience, related in "The Bishop and the Canary," was this feeling of God everywhere, not cramped into church buildings or institutions, as Emily said repeatedly. She tells of sitting fuming in a church, listening to what she describes as a mournful chant: "We beseech Thee o hear us, good Lord. . . . I longed to get out of church and crisp up in the open air. God got so stuffy squeezed into a church. Only out in the open was there room for Him. He was like a great breathing among the trees." (Shadbolt, 60)

Over and over, Emily the painter and the writer shouted aloud her joy in largeness, bigness: "Canada's vastness took my breath. The up-and-downness of the Rockies, their tops dangled in clouds, thrilled and were part of natural me. . . ." (*Growing*, 81) It is ironic that someone who so wanted to paint big canvasses, explore the vastness of Canada, and in general aspired to largeness should so have identified herself with a narrator and, some have called it, "muse" named Small.

Shadbolt describes Emily's last trip to native country, in 1928, to the Queen Charlotte Islands: "the featured forms are larger in relation to the pictured space. The totem pole, a difficult form to handle pictorially, tends to be cutoff more often and presented as a substantial mass, or it is supported from behind with a more solid screen of forest." When the poles overlap, there is a greater coherence than before. The paintings between 1928 and 1931, famous beyond the rest, are full of forests, totem poles, depicted on heavy canvasses, with deep modeling and solid forms. They are postcubist in feel, she says. (Shadbolt, 64–70)

Also in 1928, Mark Tobey, twenty years younger than Emily, gave a three-week course in her studio. And then afterwards, she sent him five dollars to come and criticize her work; he didn't come. Instead, he sent her a letter with advice, which she quotes. He has told her to "get off the monotone . . . make half-tone, one third black and white. . . . I know I am in a monotone. My forests are too monotonous. I must pep them up with higher contrasts. But what is it all without soul?" (Shadbolt, 62) None of Emily's paintings are without that.

In 1930, she lectured in Victoria, and the *Victoria Daily Times* wrote a review of the talk, on Wednesday, March 5, under the heading: "Modern art is analyzed by Miss E. Carr." A show of her work was, it pointed out, in the Crystal Garden Gallery. This noted Victorian artist, they said, is pleading for a greater tolerance toward the creative School of Canadian Modern art. She was speaking, they said, of the influence of Cézanne on modern art, "his great aim being to create forms to express the emotions that he felt for what he learned to see." Emily Carr had said that "Painters must strive to express Canada. Misty landscapes and gentle cows do not express Canada—even the cows know that." (Archives, Emily Carr)

Also in 1930, she began to keep in her notebooks the history of her being and the story of her paintings: began "to jot me down in, unvarnished me, old at 58." She wrote this on November 3, 1930, and it is these journals, which she did not publish but left behind, edited by Ira Dilworth later as *Hundreds and Thousands: The Journals of an*

Artist. In these journals, which have been considerably tidied up, we read the stories of her boarding house and her travels, her disappointments with her critics and her friends, and her various elations. To compare these journals with the tales she published in her lifetime (in which her writing can be said to fall between the years of 1937 and 1941) is instructive about what you leave out and what you transform in order to tell a story.

Her stories are strong indeed. They remind me of the way in which she described the discourse between the two stuffed eagles in her bedroom: "strong talk," the sort of talk the figures on totem poles exchanged. Much is odd about them, as much was odd about her. For one thing, her adopted persona, called "Small," presides over a great many things long after a wee person becomes a grownup—in Emily, still angry, still irritable, still idealistic in many ways, Emily who finds God in the natural world all around and waxes lyrical on the slightest occasion, there remains Small, never about to grow up. After "The Book of Small," on the basis of a 1934 draft, there remains "Growing Pains: An Autobiography," whose title indeed indicates the adult-information, but whose tales have not the power of her paintings. What writing could?, we might ask. What could possibly have the soaring height of her forests, her totem poles, her mountains, all in their rhythmic swirling?

All the same, the journals have very often something of the flavor of the out of doors. They are about intensity, that intensity of the everyday she so cared about. They are about the wonders of camping in her van, the Elephant, about her surroundings and her faith, about her rebellion against the stuffy politeness of Victorian Canada, against the social realm in which painters often have to move to create and save their reputation, sell their paintings, and the rest. From the beginning, she had found Victoria of a slowness truly remarkable. Writing to the director of the National Gallery in Ottawa, she had announced, in no uncertain terms: "I think Victoria is the most hopeless place in the Dominion." And later, she was always to complain about the lack of understanding she met. Her critics leapt upon this refusal to conform to anything society would have demanded with all their claws bared: I am thinking in particular of "Dionysius" whose savage attack was about as racist as was possible, saying that someone who lived too close to the primitive peoples of a region was likely to be contaminated by their thinking, to become "like them." This was the same attitude that was responsible for the supremely odious terminology applied to her paintings: "these atrocities."

But here is the sad thing. She never, no matter what praise was bestowed, felt sufficiently recognized: "If the work had been big enough—hit the bulls'-eye—people would *have* to acknowledge it." (Shadbolt, 14) But it was big enough, it was monumental. It was epic. Was she right, reflecting on her own part in all of this?

When, in February of 1936, she was about to give up being a land-lady and the necessity of earning her living that way, she wrote about her own relation to those who would have helped her: "things were suggested, but I let them slip, was saucy over them . . . I did not push. Praise embarrassed me so that I wanted to hide. You've got to meet success half-way. I wanted it to come all the way, so we never shook hands."

It seems to me that large part, perhaps the major part of her think-ing herself not enough recognized is ascribable to her general tem-perament of irritability. In a sense, her cutting herself off in later years had to do with her deafness. But in any case, in the long run, she separated herself even from erstwhile close friends like Lawren Harris, with whom she ceased to correspond in 1939, when she was sixty-nine because of his theosophist beliefs, yes, but also from some innate need of isolation—she had no one. Harris went to teach at Dartmouth College, and then to Santa Fe. As she had exulted at one point over the western part of Canada being so isolated, so her own laments over her own isolation are themselves more about irritation than self-pity. She had always preferred animals to people, trees to polite civilization. And perhaps as a result, when she was elderly, she was feeling her loneliness; but she had really felt it all along: "I haven't one friend of my own age and generation. I wish I had. I don't know if it's my own fault. I haven't a single thing in common with them. . . . None of them like painting and particularly dislike my kind of painting. . . . Oh Lord, I thank thee for the dogs and the monkey and the rat." And, after reading Gertrude Stein's *Autobiography of Alice B. Toklas*:

Oh, if there was only a really kindred spirit to *share* it with, that we might keep each other warm in spirit, keep step and tramp uphill together. I'm a bit ashamed of being a little depressed again. Perhaps it is reading the autobiography of Alice. B. Toklas—all the artists there in Paris, like all the artists in the East, jogging along, discussing, con-demning, adoring, fighting, struggling, enthusing, *seeking* together, jostling each other, instead of solitude, no shelter, exposed to all the "winds" like a lone old tree with no others round to strengthen it against the buffets with no waving branches to help keep time. . . . It must be my fault somewhere, this repelling of mankind and at the same time rebelling at having no one to shake hands with but myself. . . . Stop this yowl and go to your story and enter the joy of the birds. Wake the old sail up, hoist it up in the skies on lark songs. Lay the foundations strong and flat and coarse on the croaks of the crows and the jays and the rooks. Fill it with thrush songs and blackbirds, and when the day is petering out wrap the great white owl's silent wings round it and let the nightingale sing it to sleep. (Complete Writings, 733)

But she had always been lonely, not just alone: "I wonder will death be much lonelier than life. Life's an awfully lonesome affair. . . . You come into the world alone and you go out of the world alone yet it seems to me you are more alone while living than even coming and going." (July 16, 1933, Journals, 41)

Reading an artist's journal can be revealing of more than the paintings—and yet of painting also. We learn of her techniques for making her most famous oil-on-paper works: she bought cheap manila paper in large sheets, tore them into smaller surfaces, and painted with ordinary white house paint mixed with the more expensive pigment, thinned down with gasoline. This way, she could afford to paint. She liked to sketch outside and then, as with fresh food, "Carry it right home and use it."

Here are a few of Emily's reflections in 1933, about her mountains—for her paintings make them hers: "mountains towering—snow mountains, blue mountains, green mountains, brown mountains, tree-covered, barren rock, cruel mountains with awful waterfalls and chasms and avalanches, tender mountains all shining. . . ." Wrestling with one of her mountains, she would generally sit in front of it for hours and only then "realize it fiercely, vitally." (August 7, 1933, Journals, 47) Either she feels swept up in the melody of where she is—like the swirls of her forests and mountains that sweep you in—or then, as she so succinctly laments on some occasions: "I don't know the song of this place." (September 9, 1933, Journals, 56) To not know it from the inside toward the surface, the way Indian art taught her to know things, to have not had that necessary experience, means the representation will lack the point, as with the hapless painter Emily described, looking once at a weak watercolor. This teaches a lesson in strong art talk:

The objects, water, sky, rocks, were there but he hadn't felt that they were big or strong or high or wet.

I want my things to rock and sway with the breath and fluids of life. . . . I myself have not swayed and rocked with experience when I confronted them. It was but their outer shell; I did not bore into them, reach for their vitals. . . . (July 25, 1933, Journals, 45)

Generally, it seems to me, she did reach for the vitals of what she painted, and generally grasped them.

One of her most notable dreams was about greenness and grow-ingness. It explains some of her extraordinary forest works, in which, as she said, each tree has to be related to each other. But here she speaks about the actual growing process, on a wooded hillside. Unlike ordinary woods, this one is stronger and more ardent: "But, in my dream that hillside suddenly lived—weighted with sap, burning green in every leaf, every scrap of it vital." (*Growing*, 262)

Irresistible, her description of sketching, at an advanced age, in her beloved woods.

. . . being elderly, you spread your camp stool and sit and look around. "Don't see much here." "Wait." Out comes a cigarette. The mosquitoes back away from the smoke. Everything is green. Everything is waiting and still. Slowly things begin to move, to slip into their places. Groups and masses and lines tie themselves together. . . . Nothing is crowded; there is living space for all. . . . Life is sweeping through the spaces. Everything is alive. The air is alive. . . . Light and dark chase each other. . . . You must be still in order to see. (Complete Writings, 794)

All her life, it was her art and her writing, and her writing about paint-ing that concerned her most. Queried shortly before she died about the "outstanding events" in her life, she responded: "work and more work!" Here, we remember Suzanne Valadon asking a friend at her last exhibition: "Well, are you working?" and, when he answered, "Like you, alas, with less joy!" her remonstrating: "Be quiet, work's the only thing that matters."

In October of 1935, she gave a well-received lecture at the Provincial Normal School, later published as "The Something Plus in a Work of Art." In it, she insists on what the Japanese call *Sei Do*, that is, "the transfusion into the work of the *felt nature* of the thing to be painted." (Blanchard, 251) There was a large audience, and she was curious about the reaction among the young people. Her reflection directly after the talk is as much about reaching out as her paintings had been: "If ever I speak again, I'm going to try and face up to my audience squarer, to take courage to let my eyes go right over them to the very corners of the room, and feel the space my voice has to fill and then to meet all those bright young eyes." (October 19, 1935, Journals, 203)

This year of 1935, she was holding shows of her work in her house at Simcoe Street, attended by other bright young eyes, and older ones, and she was also sketching outdoors. But that had to be given up, and, in 1936, when she was sixty-four, she settled into a cottage in Victoria's James Bay, on Beckley Avenue, at No. 316, not far from her sisters. Here she had both sunlight and sea.

In 1937 she had a heart attack, then another in 1939, but she continued to paint. Her four paintings exhibited at the Tate Gallery's 1938 exhibition "A Century of Canadian Art" were widely remarked on in the press. She had other exhibitions, at the Crystal Garden in Victoria, at the Island Arts and Crafts Society, and she would open her studio at times. Not all the experiences of visitors were positive. Here, from the archives, is a jotting on September 17, which Ira Dilworth thought better not to include in the published journals—we can see why.

> Mrs. Lemoine Fitzgerald came—no like. They all lie grovelling in adoration before Lemoine. She asked to see pictures and then looked at the ceiling and the rag rugs which she admired greatly—a nasty woman. Used yellow red rouge which sat badly. Had a very pretty striped necktie and a fool of a relation tagging along. The pair made me good and all round sick.

There was a certain amount of recognition: On May 7, 1938, she went to a university womens' garden annual meeting at the University of British Columbia, and exclaimed later to herself:

> What rubbish they talked. All sinking in a garrulous flutter of elderness. All the women were *very* ugly and the garden charming . . . they were wrinkled, hardfaced, marcelled and uninteresting. Thin brains had not made them lovely though the *president* did have charm & no frills. They gave Dr. Ryan a corsage because she was such an old useful member & me one because I was new. And had no brain like the rest. I felt as if I got the booby prize but it was kind & it was the first function I'd taken in for 18 months. (Archives ms. 2763, box 1)

It is not difficult to see why this entry as well was not included by Ira Dilworth in the journals.

She was plagued by headaches and chest pains, but continued working. She would go to tea at the Empress Hotel to meet artists, taking her budgerigars in aviary boxes, and would go to sketch and try to get into her painting the "heavy woods movement" she saw and felt. In the fall, there was to be the first of her annual solo exhibitions at the Vancouver Art Gallery. This time, there were twenty-seven paintings. But her worry about being shown to the public was great. The paintings would reveal

> my thoughts my way of seeing. People who know me & people who don't are going to stare at my innards criticise jeer love, hate, smile, praise, announce. I shall be set up in the market place for the public to do to me what it wants. I'm glad not to be there, but it is cowardly too not to face myself for the woods mirrored me before I while I sat looking . . . (October 4)
> My show opened in the Vancouver Gallery. I've stood naked before all those eyes. They judged me found me wanting ridiculed me loved me wondered about me some have been jealous some scornful. I don't care. Alice does not care either she's never asked a word about the show her only interest possible *sales*. I feel a complete failure. (October 12)

On October 15, she is worrying about how people took the show, "despite there having been a "write up rather less repulsive than usual. Said I got nearer the heart of B[ritish] C[olumbia]. than any other painter." But still, "one's fizz goes flat." Part of the issue is, of course, that no one in her family seems to take any interest at all. To follow Emily's day by day reaction is to feel just what the strain between her and her family must have been. As she had said before, "Art was taboo in the family. My kind was considered a family disgrace." So her reaction to Alice's not caring was intense:

> Oct. 16: I think one must always feel a bit flattened by a show. Of course my nieces or anyone belonging to me did not go it would not occur to them or to write me if they did go. A[lice] has never mentioned show or asked a thing about it since the crates went away. I expect she's forgotten all about it I couldn't show her the press notices I just couldn't. Perhaps it's just vanity. My self-conceit makes me feel bad A[lice]. couldn't make herself enthusiastic or proud. . . .
> Oct 17 Donals in Vancouver enthusiastic beyond measure about my show Letter also from Vancouver Gallery pleased with attendance. Letter from May Coleman also delighted. I cried hard over my mail. A[lice]. rang up and asked if I heard anything of show. Was very angry when rung up by Mary Lawrson who told her she *ought* to have gone

over with me. She said she could go this weekend if I wanted. I said no. I had written already to say I would *not* be over.

Oct 18. Lawren sent 10 dollars for trip if I wanted to go up and couldn't see why I wanted Alice to go up too—thought I should not expect A[lice] to go. . . . Tired and down hearted cried off and on through the day don't know *why* I feel so low. . . . I could not say my relations along with the exhibition would make me sick—don't mix.

Oct 19 Decided to go to Vancouver *alone*. A furious about it. Worked on blouse.

Oct. 20. Go to Vancouver tomorrow A. *very* put out because I am going alone. It is much best so but feel awful to have her so hurt and angry when I go.

. . . Edith says "It has always surprised me how the untutored artistically respond to your work. Of herself and husband she writes" there has never been anything at the gallery that has meant so much to us." Glorious day

When Emily returned home, Alice was still wrathful. And so it went. Emily's self-portrait of 1938 shows her familiar headband, set mouth, and firm eyes: she knew what she was about.

Eventually Emily had to abandon her beloved cottage on Beckley Street, because of the expense of it, and in 1940, she moved. It was very hard to leave behind a "space that has enclosed your own peculiarities for a while." And then, there were the problems with her sister. "Alice is hurt so easily and I am rather clumsy, I fear." (Journals, Feb. 8, 1940, 316)

Moving in with Alice, in 1940, at 218 St. Andrew's Street, must have been no picnic, as the expression goes, certainly not like the comradeship she had experienced with her mother so long ago, on that real picnic among the lilies.

Yet here is the last entry in Emily's journal, and it is about persistence, about the same kind of bursting through that we recognize in one of her first entries in *Growing Pains*, about her father's pride. Emily Carr had her pride also, and it enabled much. Her stories were beginning to be read on CBC radio, and this was a good moment: "spring bursts through as strong as ever. I gave the birds their mates and nests today. They are bursting their throats. Instinct bids them carry on. They fulfill their moment; carry on, carry on, carry on." (March 7, 1941, Journals, 332)

And she did also carry on. I think Emily Carr's work and life might be best summed up by one of her reflections, when she returned to the west of Canada from England—for in a sense, all her work was just that, a return to the coast she so loved, and to which her own work bears the greatest testimonial. This was just the place "her voice had to fill," and it finally did part that.

It was good to stand in space. (*Growing*, 204)

CHAPTER 5

PAULA MODERSOHN-BECKER

REQUIEM FOR A FRIEND

It seems to me terribly difficult to live one's life to its end in a good and great way . . .

—*Paula's Journal (May 2, 1902, 277)*

It was a very brief life, only from 1876 to 1907, 31 years. Paula Becker, the wife of Otto Modersohn, had only 3 years of study, and 7 years in which she produced her work, making some 560 paintings, 700 drawings, and 13 etchings. She only sold 3 or 4 paintings—two to Clara Westhoff and Rainer Maria Rilke, who were her close friends, and two to the Heinrich Vogelers, friends from the small painter's colony at Worpswede, where she lived much of her life and where she died.

The tragic end, briefly sketched, is that toward the end of her life she had made her fourth trip to Paris, hoping this time to get on seriously with her painting, and planning to leave her husband, Modersohn. At one point, he came to Paris, she became pregnant, and, after they returned to Worpswede, she gave birth to her daughter, and died shortly thereafter, saying "A pity." Many of her paintings were left unfinished.

Modersohn-Becker abounded in pictures of the Worpswede peasants, of nature, and of maternity, before which she pictured herself as kneeling "in humility." But, says Whitney Chadwick, "her diary records her ambivalence towards marriage, motherhood, and art." (Chadwick, 287) The terrible irony of the woman painter celebrating all those images of fecundity of 1906 and 1907 and then dying soon after her own giving birth casts its own shadow over this story.

What she left behind, apart from her work, is a quite extraordinary collection of letters and journals. The style and the vision are captivating, as intense as if she were speaking to you as well as herself, and are totally engaged in her ongoing struggle with her work and life.

Part of the interest of the story is the clash between Paula's bourgeois background and her bohemian, artistic form of life. She was born Paula Becker in Dresden into a cultured family. Her father, an official with the German railway, was unimpressed by the idea that she might want to be a painter, and especially unconvinced that she would add up to anything by devoting herself to such a calling. (Women get married and have children: art school is not helpful toward this end.) The family moved, in 1888, to Bremen, near which was the Worpswede colony that would so mark her life and work.

Following her father's urging, she began a teacher training course in 1893, and began finally a course in art, under his disapproving eye, in 1896, at the Berlin School of Art for Women. Here it was the portrait classes of Jeanne Bauck, as well as Bauck's personality, that especially inspired her.

And then, to Worpswede, where she studied with Fritz Mackenson, and met Otto Modersohn, twelve years older than she, of a relatively timid character and more conservative in his painting than Paula would prove to be. But how she loved Worpswede! Worpswede, a small artist's colony, twelve and one-half miles northeast of Bremen, was modeled on the experience of the artist's colony at Barbizon, in the forest outside Paris. It was founded by Fritz Mackensen, Otto Modersohn, Fritz Overbeck, Hans am Ende, and Heinrich Vogeler, and was for a time a center of enthusiastic community living and painting. There were classes, gatherings, and mutual encouragement. In this rural community, there were evenings spent together in Vogeler's house, called the Barkenhoff, and the writers Gerhart Hauptmann and Rilke were regular visitors. The high point of the colony, the era of its greatest glory, was around the year 1900 and shortly thereafter, which coincides with Paula's most crucial work and legend. She loved it with the kind of passion that you see in her paintings of the Worpswede peasants and fields: "Worpswede, Worpswede, Worpswede! . . . Birches, birches, pines and old willows. The beautiful brown moor, delicious brown! The canal boats with their dark sails . . . .Worpswede, Worpswede, you are always on my mind. . . . Your mighty grandiose pines!" (12)

This passage, from 1897, is characteristic of her enthusiastic approach to the colors that drench all the most characteristic

Worpswede landscapes: browns of all huesi; greens, bright and duller: and the very particular dark shadows you might see as gloomy or then as picturesque. (On one wall of my house, as I was growing up, was a reproduction of one of these deep-hued landscapes, imbued with melancholy. My grandmother would say, like Paula, "Worpswede . . ." and then lapse into silence. Having no especial idea of what those three syllables meant, I found them to be a kind of magical formula. They have remained that and more.)

How beautiful it all must have seemed. Paula's journal from October 4, 1898, reads like a witness to joy:

> I walked through the darkened village. The world lay back around me, deep black. It seemed as if the darkness were touching me, kissing, caressing me. I was in another world and felt blessed where I was. For it was beautiful. Then I came back to myself and was still happy, for everything here was also beautiful and dark and soft like a kind and grown-up person. And the little lights shone in the houses and laughed from the windows out onto the street and at me. And I laughed back, bright and joyful and grateful. I am alive. (109)

This reminds me of Emily Carr's frequent exultation over the "the alive in us, in a feeling I find characteristic of all these women.

Over and over, the wording of Paula's thoughts seems to me to confer that kind of depth on her painting that the very best of journals is able to bring about. She is given to writing in the parable mode, exemplified by this meditation, Gemanic-sentimental, like much Worpswede painting:

> I should like to create pious figures with soft and blissful smiles, figures wandering through green fields, along riverbanks. Everything should be pious and good. And I love color. . . . Everything around me glows with passion. Every day reveals a new red flower, glowing, scarlet red. Everyone around me carries them. Some wear them quietly hidden in their hearts. And they are like poppies just opening, of which one can see only here and there a hint of red petal peeking out from the green bud.
>
> And others carry them in pale, soft hands, walking slowly in their trailing garments and keeping their gaze fixed on the ground. They are waiting for the wind that will come and bend their red flower, so that it will kiss in one flame.
>
> And there are others. They swagger along with their heads held high. They strip the blossoms and break them, and go on their drunken way. Which of these is life? the true life? (M, 152)

—Paula's own moral sense was strong, and her passion for looking and being and creating no less so.

In 1898, Paula spent some time in Berlin, then established herself in Worpswede, where she met Clara Westhoff, also a painter, who was to be always her best friend. Over and over, in the times they spent at Worpswede or in Paris, or when Clara was married to Rilke and Paula to Otto, up until the early end of Paula's life, it was Clara who mattered.

In 1899, Paula was shown for the first time in the Bremen Kunsthalle Worpswede exhibition. And in 1900, she made her first trip to Paris, where she studied at the Académie Colarossi, and took an anatomy class at the Ecole des Beaux Arts, where women had only recently been admitted. Her studio was at 9, Campagne Première, a street now celebrated in art history for Man Ray's having worked and lived there. She met Emil Nolde, some of whose "unpainted paintings" in Siebull resemble some of Paula's own work—the flat fields and dulled colors, the windmills, the canals—and saw a good deal of Clara, who lived in the same hotel on the Boulevard Raspail, and who was studying sculpture with Rodin. They went to exhibitions together, and copied paintings in the Louvre. It was with Clara that she saw Cézanne's works at Ambroise Vollard's gallery, which made a clear mark on her own imagination and work.

Clara and Paula returned to Worpswede, and spent the next winter together in Berlin. Back in Worpswede, Otto's wife Helen died. Rilke was then in Worpswede, where Paula saw a good deal of him—clearly there was an attraction between them. It was to Rilke that Paula announced her engagement to Otto, and to him that she frequently wrote, as to Clara, about her emotions. Rilke and Clara married in 1901, and Paula felt the lack of her friend greatly. Clara has gone her own way, wrote Rilke to Paula, and complained that Clara only spoke of work, work work. Just as Rodin had said to both the Rilkes, "Travailler, toujours travailler." (Letters, 345)

Then in 1902, in preparation for her marriage, Paula went to cookery school in Berlin. This was not a time that was of great joy to her, but she wrote copiously to her great redbearded friend, Otto. Painting she preferred to cookery. Back in Worpswede in March, she married Otto, on May 25 of 1902.

It seemed to be fine at first. Directly after their marriage, Otto reflected on her qualities, for which, we presume, he married her. The two seem to have had much in common, from his initial point of view, which he states in outline style. To compare their two journal styles is already to see a great division, between her lyric flowing style and his Teutonic dryness. Here he outlines her character:

1. Artistic Person
purely personal ideas on art, painting, literature (music) enjoyment and creation of art her main objective—and mine.
Nature, country life, Worpswede, old houses, old establishments etc. like me
2. Free Person
lets herself go regardless. Cheerful, lively fresh temperament. Compensates for mine, that's what I particularly like.
3. Outward charming, sweet, strong, healthy, energetic (M, 26).

Sounds all right. But the cheerful and lively and energetic Paula, side by side with his gloomy temperament for which hers was to compensate, seemed not to find it an especially joyous situation:

I have cried a lot in my first year of marriage . . . I feel lonely as I did in my childhood . . . It is my experience that marriage does not make one happier. It destroys the illusion that has been the essence of one's previous existence, that there existed something like a soul-mate. The feeling of not being understood is heightened in marriage by the fact that one's entire life before hand had the aim of finding a being who would understand one. But isn't it better to exist without such an illusion and look this great lonely truth straight in the eye? (M, 33)

Yet, she continues, this straightforward looking may not be all bad. Art deepens, and female friendships make up for the difficulties of marriage. But it is all so hard.

The loneliness sometimes makes me sad, and sometimes, happy. I believe it makes me a deeper person. . . . we live turned toward the inside. . . . And then I've had this experience: my heart has been longing for a certain soul, whose name is Clara Westhoff. I think we shall never again find each other completely. We are on different paths. And maybe this loneliness is good for my art. . . . Blessed, blessed, blessed. (M, 33)

Art is what counts. And that is what she cared most about. Painting, painting, painting. On June 3, after this Easter vision, she was still caring about exactly that: "Someday I must be able to paint truly remarkable colors. Yesterday I held in my lap a wide, silver-gray satin ribbon which I edged with two narrower black, patterned silk ribbons. And I placed on top of these a plump, bottle-green velvet bow. I'd like to paint something one day in those colors." (M 278) More than the content, the vibrancy of the coloration matters—this is clearly a painter writing.

In her journal of the same year, 1902, we can see her observing self taking shape. Each passage contributes to the overall truthfulness of her own interior portrait of herself. For Paula was above all a painter, despite her domestic longings—she describes the house she wants to build, with low windowsills to sit on, partly between the outside and the in, with nooks and crannies everywhere. Yet, here she is mostly herself, and again the colors and the shapes and the shadows are what matter: "When I'm talking to someone I observe diligently what kind of shadow the nose is throwing and how the deep shadow on the cheek stands out strongly and then melts into the light."

But Otto, understandably perhaps, as a painter living alongside a painter less famous than himself was not thrilled by her exalted state of painterly enthusiasm. For his temperament was completely other. He summed up her characteristics, now in a less kind manner. They probably had not changed, but the "compensation" they were to enact against his more gloomy self had not always been efficacious. Paula had perhaps been a bit too energetic and caring about her own art. This is exactly where the crisis point will be, between their personalities.

He is writing this in February, and they have only been married a short while:

February 28, 1902
Unfortunately, Paula has been infected by modern notions. She is also quite accomplished in the realm of egotism. Whoever is not deep enough or fine enough in her estimation is pushed aside gruffly and ruthlessly. . . . I , too, have already and frequently been the object of this gruff egotism. I wonder whether all gifted women are like that?

It must be the most difficult thing for a woman to be highly developed spiritually and to be intelligent, and still be completely feminine. These modern women cannot really love; or they grab hold of love only from the animalistic side of their nature, and the psyche has no part in it. . . . With all their intelligence, they get further and further away from any goal. They think that egotism, independence, conceit , are the best things there are; and no happy marriage can come from that. The husband, naturally, is caught up in medieval , tyrannical appetites if he expects his wife to do him favors, live with him, enter into his interests. To do that, of course, a wife would have to sacrifice her rights and her personality. (M, 281)

We have seen the difference between Paula's father's point of view about her art and her own: now it is clear that this was no less true of her husband. During their lifetimes, Otto was the successful painter. So this is where the tragedy of non-recognition comes in, and where we see the male judgement of female work: how else to put it? Rilke will at a later point be part of this camp also, before writing the poem which gives its title to this chapter.

Then, in 1903, Paula returned to her beloved Paris, and spent from February to March there, frequenting Rodin's studio, as did so many enraptured female painters and sculptors, like Camille Claudel. Not only female artists, of course: Rilke served as Rodin's secretary for a while, and some of his poems from that period were written in French.

Paula loved Paris: writing her journal at the Grand Hôtel de la Haute Loire, room 53, she exults, on February 10: "Wherever I go, champagne is in the air, not to speak of all the art one sees wherever one goes."

> I welcome the spring outside with passion. It must consecrate me and my art. It will strew flowers on me as I work. I found coltsfoot out by the brickyard. I carried some of them around with me and held them up to see how the yellow stood out deep and shining against the sky.

Ten days later, she writes in her journal:

> I must learn how to express the gentle vibration of things, their rough-ened textures, their intricacies. I have to find an expression for that in my drawing, too, in the way I sketch my nudes here in Paris, only more original, more subtly observed. The strange quality of expectation that hovers over muted things. (M, 299)

And here she mentions those things, such as skin, Otto's forehead, fabrics, and flowers, adding:

> it's in my blood to want to overdo things. . . . To get back again to that "roughened intricacy of things": that's the quality I find so pleasing in old marble or sandstone sculptures that have been out in the open, exposed to the weather. I like it, this roughened, alive surface. (M, 299)

And then, on the 17th of the same month, she moves to 24, rue Cassette, loving her new quarters as she loved the old.

In 1905, Paula returned to Paris for the third time, and visited classes at the Académie Julian taking a special interest in the work of Edouard Vuillard, Maurice Denis, and Pierre Bonnard. For the fourth time, leaving Worpswede and determined to separate from Otto and become a painter in Paris, she returned in 1906 in mid-February, had an atelier on the Boulevard Montparnasse, again visited anatomy classes at the Ecole des Beaux-Arts, and saw a good deal of work by Manet and Gauguin. It was a good time to be in Paris for Paula especially, who had a foreboding:

> I am becoming something—I am living the most intensely happy time of my life.
>
> I know I shall not live very long. But why is that so sad? Is a festival more beautiful because it lasts? My sensuous perceptions grow sharper, as if I were supposed to take in everything within the few years that will be offered to me. . . . And now love will still blossom for me before I depart, and if I've painted three good pictures, then I shall leave gladly with flowers in my hand and my hair. (M, 35)

She did have them both, love and art. This is the turning point Rilke has described, saying that her work is so splendid, but her ruminations so fragmentary and doing her no credit: these ruminations are about the wish to be alone, to be free of the domination of a husband, who so wanted a child. She wanted one also, but not yet, not yet, as she continued to say.

But Otto came to Paris in June, and again in the autumn, wanting to hold on to his marriage, and to have a child with her. They exhibited together in the Bremen Kunsthalle, and saw the Cézannes in the Pellerin Collection. In 1907 they returned to Worpswede, with Paula pregnant and determined to keep up both her family life and her painting. Rilke's letters to Clara about Cézanne, which Clara had sent to her, were among the last things she read. She gave birth to her daughter on November 2, and then, on November 21, the final tragedy occurred. Now Rilke can read this as her "leaving us with beauty," but the event remains open to interpretation.

Clara recounted the scene, as Paula got out of bed, and saw herself:

> in the large mirror placed at the foot of her bed and combed and braided her hair, and wound the braids into a crown around her head. She pinned roses which someone had sent her to her dressing gown , and when her husband and brother were preparing to support her on either side, she gently walked ahead of them into the other room. There, candles had

been lighted everywhere in the chandelier, on a garland of candle holders around the body of a carved baroque angel, and in many other places. She then asked for her child to be brought to her. When this was done she said," It's almost like Christmas. . . . Oh, I'm so happy, so happy!" Suddenly her feet seem to become heavy, there were a few gasps for breath. She said softly, "A pity," . . . and died. (M, 537)

There were indeed flowers in her hair, roses here, as she had predicted, and we recall her self-portrait with a camellia branch from an earlier time. On her easel remained a painting of sunflowers, unfinished.

What Paula had said of herself in 1902 sticks in my mind as the best summing up of her life, beautiful in its exaltation of art. Here is what mattered to her: "soon the time will come when I won't need to be ashamed and keep quiet but I shall feel with pride that I am a painter." (Journal, 139)

The story line is very strong, and the power of it has itself given birth to two poems: one by Adrienne Rich, written like a letter from Paula to Clara Westhoff, her friend; and, nearer in time to the occasion, Rilke's epic "Requiem for a Friend." This poem was written *after* his refusal to edit her letters and journals, a task he was invited to do and for which, one would think, he would have been ideally suited, as her friend and a great poet. Like André Gide's lack of enthusiasm for and understanding of Dorothy Bussy's short novel *Olivia*, which she had shared with him as someone who might have been expected to understand, Rilke's hesitation over and ultimate refusal of this task seems to me significant of a certain attitude, not unlike Otto's concern about Paula's "egotism" and "gruffness."

Rilke states his reasons, couched along the lines that it would do her reputation no good:

the editing (and publication) of these papers would be wrong, if for no other reason than that the picture of Paula Modersohn to which they contribute would inevitably be an indescribably inferior image to the one she ultimately attained in her final year and in the great beauty of her departure from us. Much of what was unique about her would, of course, be conveyed, but not she herself—only what was ready and waiting in her. But not her freedom, not her great productive heart, nothing of the rapid, sudden ascent which is revealed and remains preserved in the final stages of her art.

Paula's "new life," whose inception is dated February 24, 1906 knew only two things: work and fate. . . . As it is, these papers are negated, canceled out, obliterated by the artistic production of this valiant and struggling woman. . . . In her very late writings there is only the merest handful of passages that give us a taste of this change. It is in her work, the work of that ultimate, abundant year, that she attained the fulfillment which in the end decisively wins us over to her. (M, 539)

Paula, he said, was not always truthful in what she wrote, and a certain "compromising nature" was evident in her writings. "Concerned, indeed, worried about being charming and gracious" at first, and then "ruthlessly independent," her life and writings show an "astonishing tension between validity and grace" (539), and her journals fail to reveal much about her later experience. Moreover, he says, and this astonishes the present reader far more than the contradictions Paula had to live through and express: "Ever since the two volumes of van Gogh's letters and journals were made available to us . . . and as a consequence any recounting of the experience of being a painter which is less complete or less passionate than van Gogh's is rendered ineffectual by the very existence of his writings." (538) !!!

A half-year later, in the summer of 1917, Rilke was still thinking over the problem, and concluded: "it may simply be that her final years were too short to permit any articulation whatsoever alongside the breathless progress of her art— . . . they depreciate rather than enhance the already tenuous image and understanding of her art . . ." (M, 538–9)

I think it fair to say that many of us, her readers of her letters, journals, and art, do not agree with this interpretation, finding her articulation of both problems and progress fully worth following.

Rilke's judgment on Paula's writing—to be sure, without having had access to all of it, some being naturally withheld from him, given its occasionally harsh words about him and his marriage—has the same surprised tone as Judith Gautier's biographer marveling over her choice of a final companion: ("The woman who had once loved Catulle Mendès with passion, who had been the mistress of Hugo, the inspiration of Wagner, the love of Mohsin-Khan, the admiration of Baudelaire, Leconte de Lisle and Sargent, the woman who had enslaved Benedictus, Baudry, Armand Silvestre and innumerable other men, had now become, in her sixties, dependent on a dull, uneducated, infatuated girl.") Here, Rilke depreciates her writing in comparison with her painting, which he evaluates justly:

Quite apart from her development as a human being, how is one supposed to gather from [these documents] that we are dealing with the painter, the artist, who . . . with ever greater decisiveness welcomed the influence of . . . van Gogh, Gauguin, Cézanne, the appearance of Maillol, indeed probably even of Matisse and Henri Rousseau, and who in her increasingly bold artistic production even anticipated on occasion the work of the followers of these painters in Germany [the Expressionists]. (M, 540)

It is my contention that these writings do indeed give us the flavor of just exactly that kind of painter: in fact, of that painter herself, whose personality comes through strongly in her journal, with all her contradictions and hesitations, her exultations and despair.

To my mind, he does her more justice in his very long poem, the length of one of his Duino Elegies, and in fact, it is an elegy full of regret. He is still worrying over what to do about the telling of her life and of her development, which somehow is up to the survivors of her "stern death":

> you, who have achieved
> more transformation than any other woman.
> That we were frightened when you died . . . no, rather:
> that your stern death broke in upon us, darkly,
> wrenching the till-then from the ever-since—
> this concerns *us;* setting it all in order
> is the task we have continually before us.

He had rejected any role in that setting in order before, and is now haunted by his denial of her own writing, for she had been able, on Earth, to grasp "each Thing . . . out of your great abundance." Something about Paula's generosity (not, this time, her "graciousness and charm") has to be responded to, with equal generosity, and thus this poem, which he feels called upon to utter: "What is it that you want," it asks? And he remembers how she loved fruits and understood them:

> You set them before the canvas, in white bowls,
> and weighed out each one's heaviness with your colors.
> . . .
> And at last, you saw yourself as a fruit, you stepped
> out of your clothes and brought your naked body
> before the mirror, you let yourself inside
> down to your gaze; which stayed in front,
> immense,
> and didn't say: I am that; no: this is.

There was, he thinks, in the amber beads she wore in her most famous self-portrait, so like Gauguin, a "kind of heaviness that can't exist/in the serene heaven of paintings." Rilke's eye here, as with his majestic letters on Cézanne, surely among the most powerful writings on any painter ever, is at once meditative and totally accurate: those beads weigh, they weigh like her pregnancy, like something presaging a doom. "Why do you show me an evil omen in the way you stand?" he asks. And she sensed her fate also, even as she thought it made the festival no less festive, that it was so brief. . . . Something Rilke senses is sure. "How short your life seems . . ."

> But you yourself knew. You sat up in your childbed
> and in front of you was a mirror, which gave back
> everything. And this everything was you. . . .

Rilke's summary of Paula's life and work and fate is quite as powerful as his letters on Cézanne. He captures for her a sense of freedom within the self and within the one beloved that may have been the force behind her wish to do everything: paint and live and love. It's only that she had no time. And so he speaks for her, now. If the poet has, and we have, the sense that he is somehow overwriting her journal and letters, somehow giving utterance to what she could or did not say that would have satisfied him, for such poetry that is not too great a price.

> For *this* is wrong, if anything is wrong:
> not to enlarge the freedom of a love
> with all the inner freedom one can summon.
>   . . .
> You knew so much of all this, you were able
> to do so much; you passed through life so open
> to all things, like an early morning. I know:
> women suffer; for love means being alone;
> and artists in their work sometimes intuit
> that they must keep transforming, where they love.
>   . . .
> You had just one desire: a years-long work—
> which was not finished; was somehow never finished.
>   (Rilke, 73–87, translation Stephen Mitchell)

Adrienne Rich's poem-letter from "Paula Becker to Clara Westhoff" of 1975–76 eschews the married names of the two close artist friends—for they appear here as themselves, their intimacy the point of it all. Paula, in the beginning, feels a slowness in things, with the child inside her that she did not want—in her letters and journal pages, she has repeatedly expressed her desire to separate from Otto and to paint, paint, paint. Not this burden, not yet.

In the poem, Paula has dreamed of dying in childbirth and of Rilke's writing a requiem for her. And Clara, she says, is the only one to whom she has said that she didn't want this child—maybe someday a child but not now. It feels like a fate unwished, undeserved, and terrible: Otto sees, complacently, how she will have no time for her art, but she feels now beyond him, and sure:

> I know now the kind of work I have to do.
> It takes such energy! I have the feeling I'm
> moving somewhere, patiently, impatiently,
> in my loneliness. . . .

That loneliness was from missing Clara, and from her own marriage. Rilke had not had to worry about his work as they both had, as women:

> Which of us, Clara, hasn't had to take that leap
> out beyond our being women
> to save our work? or is it to save ourselves?

There is a photograph of them both, in front of one of Paula's paintings, and the poem reminds us of all the plans they had made, suggesting all they could have done for each other. There remains just this. It has to be enough:

> . . . Clara, I feel so full
> of work, the life I see ahead, and love
> for you, who of all people
> however badly I say this
> will hear all I say and cannot say.
> (Rich, 367–9)

1. *Portrait of Judith Gautier* by John Singer Sargent, c. 1885. Oil on canvas, 39 x 24.5 inches. Gift of Mr. and Mrs. Ernest Kanzler. Photograph © 1986 The Detroit Institute of Arts

2.   Henri de Toulouse-Lautrec, *The Hangover*, c. 1887-1888. Black ink, blue pencil, and conté crayon, 49.3 x 63.2 cm. Scala / Art Resource, NY. Musée Toulouse-Lautrec, Albi, France

3. Pierre-Auguste Renoir, *Dance in the City*, c. 1883. Oil on canvas, 180 x 90 cm. Musée National d Art Moderne, Centre Georges Pompidou, Paris, France. Photo: Erich Lessing / Art Resource, NY. Musée d Orsay, Paris, France

4. Pierre-Auguste Renoir, *Dance in the Country*, c. 1883. Oil on canvas, 180 x 90 cm. Musée National d Art Moderne, Centre Georges Pompidou, Paris, France. Photo: Erich Lessing / Art Resource, NY. Musée d Orsay, Paris, France

Suzanne Valadon
1883

5.   Suzanne Valadon, *Self-Portrait*. c. 1883. Crayon and pastel on
paper, 45 x 32 cm. CNAC/MNAM/Dist. Réunion des Musées
Nationaux / Art Resource, NY. Musée National d Art Moderne,
Centre Georges Pompidou, Paris, France. Photo: Jacqueline Hyde.
© 2005 Artists Rights Society (ARS), New York / ADAGP, Paris

6. Pierre-Auguste Renoir, *The Bathers*, 1918-1919. Oil on canvas, 110 x 160 cm. Photo: Erich Lessing / Art Resource, NY. Musée d Orsay, Paris, France

7. Suzanne Valadon, *Portrait of the Composer Erik Satie*, 1892-1893. Oil on canvas, 41 x 22 cm. Private Collection. Bridgeman-Giraudon / Art Resource, NY. © 2005 Artists Rights Society (ARS), New York / ADAGP, Paris

8.   Suzanne Valadon, *Adam and Eve*, 1909. Oil on canvas, 16.2 x 13.1 cm. CNAC/MNAM/Dist. Réunion des Musées Nationaux / Art Resource, NY. Musée National d Art Moderne, Centre Georges Pompidou, Paris, France. Photo: Jacqueline Hyde. © 2005 Artists Rights Society (ARS), New York / ADAGP, Paris

9. Suzanne Valadon, *The Casting of the Net*, 1914. Oil on canvas, 2.01 x 3.01 meters. CNAC/MNAM/Dist. Réunion des Musées Nationaux / Art Resource, NY. Musée National d Art Moderne, Centre Georges Pompidou, Paris, France. Photo: Jacqueline Hyde. © 2005 Artists Rights Society (ARS), New York / ADAGP, Paris

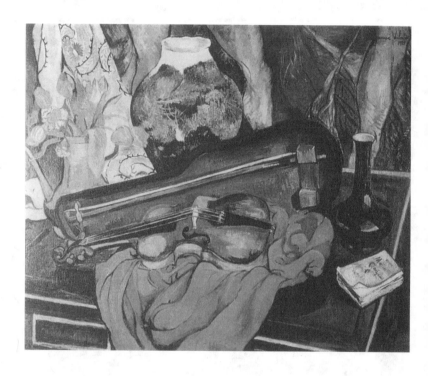

10.   Suzanne Valadon, *Still Life with Violin Case*, 1923. Oil on canvas, 81 x
100 cm. Musée Moderne d Art de la Ville de Paris. Art Resource, NY. ©
2005 Artists Rights Society (ARS), New York / ADAGP, Paris

11.   Suzanne Valadon, *The Blue Bedroom*, 1923. Oil on canvas, 90 x 116 cm. Réunion des Musées Nationaux / Art Resource, NY. Musée National d Art Moderne, Centre Georges Pompidou, Paris, France. Photo: Jacqueline Hyde. © 2005 Artists Rights Society (ARS), New York / ADAGP, Paris

12. Suzanne Valadon, *Self-Portrait with Bare Breasts*, 1931. Oil on canvas, 46 x 38 cm. Collection Bernadeau, Paris. (Photo Atelier53, Paris). Permission of Artists Rights Society. Art Resource, NY

13.   Simon Bussy, *Portrait of Dorothy Bussy*, c. 1902. Pastel, 47 x 58 cm.
Ashmolean Museum, University of Oxford

14. *Roger Martin du Gard, André Gide, Dorothy Bussy*. Breakfast at Pontigny, 1923. Association des Amis de Pontigny-Cerisy

15.   Emily Carr, *Silhouette* #2, 1930-1931. Oil on canvas, 103.2 x 86.5 cm. Collection of the Vancouver Art Gallery, Emily Carr Trust, VAG 42.3.7. Photo: Trevor Mills

16. Emily Carr, *Abstract Tree Forms*, 1932. Oil on paper, 61.1 x 91.1 cm. Collection of the Vancouver Art Gallery, Emily Carr Trust, VAG 42.3.54. Photo: Trevor Mills

17.   Emily Carr, *Wood Interior*, 1932-1935. Oil on canvas, 130.0 x 86.3 cm.
Collection of the Vancouver Art Gallery, Emily Carr Trust, VAG 42.3.5.
Photo: Trevor Mills

18. Emily Carr, *Overhead*, 1935–1936. Oil on paper, 61.0 x 91.0 cm. Collection of the Vancouver Art Gallery, Emily Carr Trust, VAG 42.3.69. Photo: Trevor Mills

19. *Photograph of Emily Carr and Flora Hamilton Burns seated on the porch of "Rat Hall."* 24 June 1939 Coll.: Toms, Humphrey. Emily Carr Archives, Parnall Collection. British Columbia Archives (Call No: C-05235)

20. *Photograph of Emily Carr standing on the porch at 316 Beckley Street, Victoria, British Columbia.* May or June 1938 Coll.: Toms, Humphrey. Emily Carr Archives, Parnall Collection. British Columbia Archives (Call No: F-05885)

21. Paula Modersohn-Becker, *Self-Portrait with Necklace*. Kunstsammlungen Bottcherstrasse, Bremen, Germany

22. Paula Modersohn-Becker, *The Sculptress Clara Rilke-Westhoff*, 1905. Oil on canvas, 52 x 36.8 cm. Bildarchiv Preussischer Kulturbesitz / Art Resource, NY. Hamburger Kunsthalle, Hamburg, Germany. Photo: Elke Walford

23. Paula Modersohn-Becker, *Self-Portrait with Hand on Chin*, 1906-1907. Oil on wood, 29 x 19.5 cm. Nieders‰chsisches Landesmuseum, Hannover, Germany

24. Paula Modersohn-Becker, *Self-Portrait with Amber Beads*, 1906. Oil on board, 62.2 x 48.2 cm. Paula Modersohn-Becker Stiftung, Bremen, Germany

25. *Photograph of Carrington, Ralph Partridge, Lytton Strachey, Oliver Strachey, and Frances Partridge.* National Portrait Gallery, London, Great Britain

26. Dora Carrington, *Portrait of Lytton Strachey*, 1916. Oil on canvas, 68.6 x 73.6. National Portrait Gallery, London, Great Britain

27. Dora Carrington, *Portrait of Gerald Brenan*, 1921. Oil on canvas, 19.5 x 16 inches. National Portrait Gallery, London, Great Britain

28.　Dora Carrington, *Farm at Watendlath*, 1921. Oil on canvas, 61.1 x 66.9 cm. Tate Gallery, London / Art Resource, NY

29.　Claude Cahun, *Self-Portrait in the Mirror with Checked Jacket*,
1928. Réunion des Musées Nationaux / Art Resource, NY. Musée des
Beaux-Arts, Nantes, France. Jersey Heritage Trust Museum

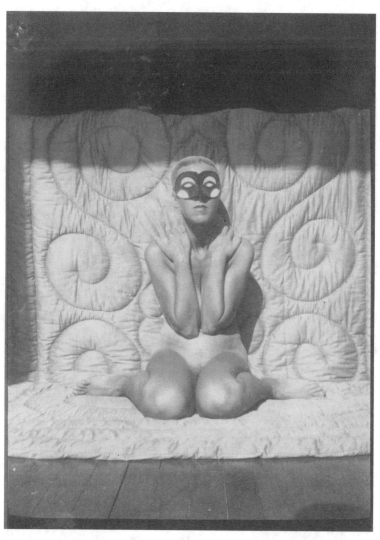

30. Claude Cahun, *Self-Portrait, Masked, Naked, Kneeling*, 1928. Jersey Heritage Trust Museum

Chapter 6

Dora Carrington

Once Upon a Time

I am not strong enough to live in this world of people, and paint.

—*Carrington, (C, 170)*

few years ago, I became involved in writing a story I cared greatly about, concerning an artist whose work and writing and life I loved. I want now to revisit it, seeing differently, from the point of view of resistance. Dora Carrington was closely associated with the Bloomsbury group, but differed from its members in significant respects, both artistically and intellectually. She is of interest not only for her painting, which was strikingly original, but for the remarkable letters and diaries that she wrote profusely, and illustrated, throughout her short life. Her artwork has the same timeless appeal, the same naive and strangely angled perception as her writings. She is also intriguing as a completely self-created person, very unlike her family and unique among the Bloomsbury group for her dress, her comportment, and her peculiar artistic vision.

Carrington lived for most of her adult life with the author Lytton Strachey, in homes that she designed and managed herself. He was thirteen years older and homosexual—their relationship seems, after a brief time of trying out the physical, to have been something else. They shared a deep bond and were central to each others' lives. The letters between them, written because they were frequently apart, are witty, affectionate, and, on Carrington's part, heartrendingly full of ups and downs of temperament. Carrington also corresponded with dozens of other friends, who cherished and saved these illustrated letters, with their misspellings and delightfully funny observations, but the letters to Lytton give the surest sense of her personality.

As a student at the Slade School of Art—where Carrington was one of the first "cropheads," those women who cut their hair short—she became involved with Mark Gertler, a painter, who fell desperately in love with her. But she insisted on her independence and refused his constant entreaties to marry him. She consented to his entreaties about lovemaking, to which a delightful missive in code—taking sugar in one's coffee and the like—bears witness. Her relation to Mark Gertler had to end, although to the regret of both. To Gertler's consternation, Carrington fell in love with Lytton Strachey, shocking Mark, because he found the soon-to-be-famous writer of *Eminent Victorians* far too elderly for Carrington, besides being clearly homosexual. Lytton, the brother of Dorothy Strachey Bussy, was, with Virginia and Leonard Woolf, and Clive and Vanessa Bell, and the painter Duncan Grant, the very center of what we have taken to calling the Bloomsbury group. So Carrington, despite her extreme difference from most of the others loosely or firmly associated with them, was continually exposed to their gatherings and ways of seeing things and persons.

She herself, although essentially a painter, had to involve herself in decorative work in order to make enough money to continue her painting and living. She did book illustration for Leonard and Virginia Woolf's Hogarth Press (Woolf and the Woolves recur frequently in her diaries and life), decorated furniture and interiors—helping Roger Fry restore the Mantegnas at Hampton Court, among other tasks—and painted pub signs. Her sense of humor prevails in all her tasks and the recounting of them, and from all accounts, her sense of joy in living was acute. She figures in texts and photographs: in Aldous Huxley's anecdotes; *Chrome Yellow* and in Mark Gertler's *Mendel*, among other novels; and in several amusing anecdotes; for example, at one of Ottoline Morell's famous Garsington weekends, she took pleasure in (and gave others pleasure by) posing as a nude statue. It was her acute delight in living, and, equally, her acute despair, these ups and downs so characteristic of all the figures in this book, that gave her life and writing such intensity. At the time of her death, just after Lytton's, Dorothy Bussy, who had thought their relation so odd before her own relation to Gide, lamented the disappearance of this "curious and fascinating personality."

Carrington's story was profoundly interwoven with other, better known stories: those of Virginia Woolf; of Woolf's sister Vanessa Bell; and of Vanessa's lovers, the magnificently enthusiastic Roger Fry, and then the grand and homosexual painter Duncan Grant. Vanessa's daughter Angelica was to call her memoir of her parents *Deceived by Kindness*, for she only learned late in life, and to her distress, that her father was Duncan after all and not Vanessa's husband Clive Bell, whose name she had been given. The man because of whom Duncan had gone to bed with Vanessa, in order to render him jealous, leaving the record of this bedding open in his diary for her to see, was the same David Garnett who was to enter Carrington's story as editor of her letters and diaries. At the birth of Angelica, he swore he would marry this child when she grew up, as he did. Then their daughter Henrietta was to marry the son of Ralph Partridge and the great lady of Bloomsbury, Frances Partridge, who had married Ralph after Carrington's suicide.

Thus the complicated plot, knotting back upon itself, and upon its tellers, might—should one want to write that kind of story—be the stuff of tragedy. So many things could be read as tragic; the love of Carrington, and Vanessa, for men who could not love them back as they would have wished, and whom they took care of almost all their adult lives; or the undervaluing of Carrington's art by the public, her friends, and herself, among others. Yet I am not choosing to read this as a tale of love doomed and of suffering, but something else entirely. Here the interpreting angle comes in. I do not believe in only one story to be told about one life, here or anywhere. Of all the tales we could tell about these three women artists, the one I am opting for is a positive one, about that energy and courage serving as the source and wellspring for the three characters in my book *Women of Bloomsbury: Virginia, Vanessa, and Carrington*, each of whom went down, in Virginia Woolf's glorious phrase: "with their colors flying." I believe that their very intensity in their creation and in their eccentric loves was integral and joined.

Interpretation is often an impassioned linking of selves and subjects, of themes and visual motifs. My story of their story contained much melodrama: two bisexuals, Virginia and Carrington, both suicides, and two women painters in love with brilliant gay creative men—Vanessa, adoring Duncan all her life, and Carrington, adoring Lytton Strachey, after whose death she waited six weeks to see if any argument could prevail against suicide, and then shot herself, wrapped in his yellow silk dressing gown.

Carrington had loved other men and women too: Henrietta Bingham with the beautiful dark hair in bangs and whom she painted naked; Ralph Partridge, whom she married because she could not be a boy and have Lytton love her; Gerald Brenan, with whom she deceived Ralph, whom Lytton loved for a while; and Beacus Penrose, far younger than herself, whose child with her she aborted. Beacus was the brother of Roland Penrose, a close friend of Roger Fry and of Picasso, and one of the main contacts between the Bloomsbury group and France.

Carrington kept a journal and wrote many letters, some of which manage to capture her "internal ecstasies" and her despairs: over her situation, so in love with someone who could not return her love equally ("my inside was as heavy as lead, as I knew how miserable it was going to be") (C, 65); and again, to Lytton: "You see I knew there was nothing really to hope for from you" (C, 175–6). She despaired over life in general ("No one but a fool imagines he can achieve happiness for more than a few months"; "No one is quite happy"; "I have very little faith in there being any happiness for human beings on this earth" (C, 246, 473); and death haunted her constantly. She lamented over her painting ("I use every excuse not to go on painting . . . the result is so amateurish and dull") (C, 465) and herself, prompt to point out her personal feelings of inadequacy. "Lytton makes me feel so stupid and hopeless about myself," she says (C, 249), and she is constantly ashamed of her "deceits and faults." (C, 229) She feels herself dull, boring: "I am unfitted to have relations with anyone." (C, 323) Ralph is eager for her to see Freud, but that does not transpire. In fact, her lucidity about her own irregularities is patent: "I am impossible" (C, 296); "I am in despair because I am against myself." (C, 317)

Of all her ups and downs, those concerned with her work seemed to capture her being most closely, for, as she says, she was never so happy as when she could paint. The extent of her imagination gave to her letters and diaries a special richness, but she lamented the fact that she was always, always thinking of so many pictures and not painting them, of caring so much about so many things. Her intensity of feeling is responsible for the veering this way and that of her moods: "Today which was so lovely, and smelt so good, suddenly by an organ grinder, made me all despair." Over and over, in her journals, she was buoyant—with living at Asheham ("Every delight seems to have congregated here") (C, 55), or just anywhere, given the particularity of detail she observed with such painterly precision: "If only there weren't so many pictures to paint, so many hills to climb, rivers to explore, letters to write, I might learn how to cook an omelette." (C, 259)

David Garnett, the editor of her *Letters and Diaries*, repeatedly points out her detestation of everything about her femaleness: "I have always hated being a woman." (C, 324) Her bisexual nature is too easily blamed for her basic inability to settle down with one person: Mark Gertler, Gerald Brenan, or Ralph Partridge. Her utter and ineradicable devotion to Lytton—how unsuitable, said Dorothy Bussy, before finding herself in the same situation, as did Vanessa Bell—is too easily blamed for her frequent unhappiness. Now it seems to me we should salute that ability to love so deeply, even as we may regret her ending her life. I do not want to take the point of view of David Garnett, who says, more or less, that she should have just pulled up her socks and gotten on with life. But, from a later point of view, why would we not see and even admire the wholeness of her emotion?

Garnett detects that "almost the same deceptions, excuses and self-accusations are repeated in each relationship. And in each it was the hatred of being a woman which poisoned it." (C, 12) He lingers over her "continual deceptions and imbroglios," blames too her inability to choose for her frequent breaks and needs to restore a relation she has broken off, and finds her adoration of Lytton a classic case of attachment to a father figure. (She is given to signing her early letters to him "votre grosse bébé Carrington" and the like.) Blaming herself for things, as she often did, was not likely, he says, to improve matters. But, to give Garnett credit, he also blames the men in her life for not championing her art: unlike Duncan Grant supporting Vanessa Bell's painting, neither Mark nor Gerald, not even Lytton felt inclined to help Carrington in her work. Roger Fry remained lukewarm. When Carrington lamented to Mark that she was making a mess of her life, given what she wanted to do, and how disappointed she was in her work ("I feel so good, so powerful before I start and then when it's finished, I realise each time, it is nothing but a failure") (C, 23), he continued to believe that women should take care of men, who always do the real painting.

But Carrington had, marvelously, a true capacity for appreciating others, a great gift. When she had just gone for a walk with Alix Strachey, she returned, saying, "I think I admire her more than any human being I have ever known. Her intellectual, and moral honesty is so remarkable." And see her early salute to Ralph Partridge, whom she was eventually to marry. She speaks of him in a letter to Lytton, July 4, 1918:

> The young man Partridge . . . I found P. shared all the best views of democracy and social reform, wine and good cheer and operas. He adores the Italians and wants after the war to sail in a schooner to the

> Mediterranean Islands and Italy, and trade in wine without taking
> much money and to dress like a brigand. I am so elated and happy. It is
> so good to find someone who one can rush on and on with,
> quickly . . . not very attractive to look at. Immensely big, full of wit
> and reckless . . . a bond of dreams and worldly things. He adores eating
> and drinking. . . .(C, 111)

She loved particular things and particular people, recounting in detail
in her letters all her delights.

My life, said Carrington "is almost entirely visual." (109) So we
have in stunning detail the sights she cared about, first, the simplest
ones—"a certain tree" in a back field. "And the beauty of the mill at
the back of the house and how once a kingfisher dived from the roof
into the stream . . ." and a gift from Gerald Brenan, with whom she
was repeatedly involved over the years.

From her bed, in Venice, overlooking the Grand Canal, on June 8,
1921, Carrington writes to Gerald how remarkable it seems to her to
have him as a friend. "I hold a theory friendship is very rarely pushed to
its ultimate end, or seldom. There is a sort of convention that in opposite sexes, that it may suddenly become 'in luv', so that it's always very
carefully kept inside its wire netting—as a matter of fact 'in luv' seldom
happens, & to love extremely, even terribly, does not hurt one. . . . Ralph
is a charming companion. I only hope I shall manage to behave
myself & not make him wretched later. I see every day I've a very
sluttish character and more self-indulgent than Oscar Wilde." (HRRC)

> I love my white shawl. You will see this summer how beautiful I will
> look in it, for you. I will see a little figure walking down the Inkpen
> Beacon; I will then rush into the house, and in a moment, a
> Botticelli nymph, in a flowered shawl will fly across hedges and dew
> ponds and treading softly on gentians will meet you. . . . I feel light
> headed today. . . . The seriousness of life has departed. . . . I may
> say all this, but *you* must not reply! (C, 287)

He mustn't reply, she says, because their relationship has to be secret.

It had not always been thus. At one point, after they had been
clearly involved, Carrington writes Gerald with the sort of enthusiasm,
to which she was always given:

> Must I shout my remarks in the evening to Lytton on the lawn for you
> to hear.

I LOVE GERALD VERY MUCH, AS MUCH as prunes, as roast duck and peas, as Venice, as crown imperials, as tulips, as Devonshire cream and raspberries, as walking on Combe Downs, as Padua, more MORE MORE MORE than all these things do I love Gerald. (C, 215)

However, here drama set in. Clare Bollard, a friend of Mark Gertler and Ralph and the Woolves, had told Ralph about the Carrington and Mark relation—because Gerald had asked her to flirt with Ralph in order to leave the ground clear for himself and Carrington. Ralph had told Leonard he must absolutely kill Gerald and even ahead on Mark about his sexual relations with Carrington, who writes Gerald of the whole thing: "something is lost that cannot be altered now. . . . The last straw was when I was trying to plant some lettuces in a Despair of wretchedness, the cats both came and sat beside me, and rubbed my hands with their faces." (217, June 10, 1922)

But all the same, it was worthwhile, Carrington continues, nothing was wasted. They never argued, their relation never "faded into something casual." And she has the terrible regret "that no one now will notice what I wear, or how I feel, that I shall no longer rush down to get letters from the post. . . ." Please burn this letter, she says, as always, with her usual panic over the others becoming conscious of her feelings or their expression. Emily Carr has this same kind of panic over any revelation of her private self to the public, as does Dorothy Bussy. (How well many a reader will understand.)

It was often Carrington's complications of personality that determined her relation to others, as she wrote to Gerald Brenan on July 19, 1925:

Thinking of you I forget all the difficulties and scenes and only remember other images of you. But looking at myself I feel only resentment at my character. . . . I see *my* complexities only bring out your worst features. I am only sorry you never knew, or so seldom, my better character. For somehow you also drag out something from me which I myself do not ever feel except with you. The irony of it is that H[enrietta] (who is a person of no importance and lacks all the proper virtues, for I can see even her, detachedly today) should have so altered my physical feelings for everyone. It was seeing her again that upset me so this spring. . . . No one is quite happy. I know quite well, how much you really matter to me, but I agree with you, after one has once had a sort of perfection in a relation, one can't put up with something different. (HRRC)

It all felt, as often in Carrington's story, impossible. Gerald would leave, and she would sink into herself again. When Gerald goes away, she says, her last "contact with an outside world" will no doubt vanish. "I shall now retreat into myself again." This is the pattern always. She has written Gerald on July 26, 1929, about this spontaneity: she was an absolute sort of person, spontaneous and entirely committed to the instant: "My chief fault, if it is one, is that when I am with a person I forget everyone else, all my other relations, & feel only this person I am with, and *these* present moments exist. I'am afraid my letters must now seem as flat as poached eggs . . . You are as some wind heavily laden with perfume, which blows from over a hill into this house, & afterwards when you have gone, it seems just a little too still without flavour . . ." (HRRC)

What she hates the worst—the way she is spoken of by others—will continue until the end of her life. This is exactly what she detests: the world outside her relationships. She loved above all secrets and private references, loved to hide things and letters and even her work, all her brief life. She was unto herself. What she most hated was her secrets or intimacy being shared. Don't show this letter, she would say. Destroy it, just the way Dorothy Bussy would say to André Gide. Even as she enjoys secret plots and will ask Gerald to put his letter inside another so Ralph or Lytton won't see it, she is still always separate from those for whom living and loving seem so easy. "I envy often amiable people, for whom it is so easy to love and simply get on." (C, 51) She will always be separate from those others, those around her in the group, better adapted to social living, and elsewhere, all the ones laughing outside in the sun, while she weeps at fate.

She was always to hate the way she felt all her friends gossiping about her. Something about that secretiveness is responsible for much in her life, the inability to feel at ease even with the people she loves. She thinks herself at fault, wanting not to be discussed with others. She writes to Gerald, on that matter. I know, she says, it's an obsession with me, but please: "Gerald, I think I am unfitted as a human being to have a relation with anyone. Sometimes I think my obsessions and fancies border on insanity. . . . In any case I think *you* are too decent a human being to be dragged into my mire. . . . Please be a little proud and do not discuss me."

Perhaps it was Carrington's obsessive secretiveness that enabled the quite extraordinary writing in "Her Book"—the diary she kept secretly—already placing herself at a remove from her own being: not "My" book, but "hers" and, moreover, spelling her married name not as

Partridge, which it was, but as Partride, leaving out a letter. This double distancing is no doubt appropriate. Here she herself made herself *other*. She was distant enough to permit her lucidity about her struggles — with herself, her relations, and her work. Such clarity she brings to everything she sees. On April 13, 1917, she notes the event of having to tell Mark that she will be with Lytton. The dramatic dialogue she constructs is like that of Dorothy Bussy in her private writing:

> Will you live with him?
> No.
> But he may love you.
> No he will not. (C, 63)

There is a doubleness built in to all her reflections: I and the other; needed and loved and unloving. "How very much I cared for him suddenly came upon me. The unreality, and coldness of Lytton." (C, 63)

The conversation continues in that diary entry, with another staging recounted. Lytton and Carrington are sitting by the fire, and Lytton has asked her to describe the scene in which she had to tell Mark about their involvement. She had, she says, written him a letter saying she was in love with Lytton. Aren't you being rather romantic, asks Lytton, and are you certain?

> (L) But it's too incongruous. I'm so old and diseased. I wish I was more able.
> (C) That doesn't matter.
> (L) What do you mean? What do you think we had better do about the physical?
> (C) Oh I don't mind about that.
> (L) That's rather bad. You should. I thought you did care. What about those boys, when you were young.
> (C) Oh that was just being young. Nothing
> (L) But do you mind me being rather physically attracted?
> (C) I don't think you are really.
> (L) Why? Because of your sex?
> (C) Yes, partly. I don't blame you. I knew it long ago and went into it deliberately.
> (L) They will think I am to blame.
> (C) They needn't know.
> . . .
> (L) But my dear aren't you being rather romantic. You see I'm so very ancient, and well—

(C) It's all right. It was my fault. I knew what I was doing.

. . .

Then he sat on the floor with me and clasped my hands in his and let me kiss his mouth, all enmeshed in the brittle beard and my inside was as heavy as lead, as I knew how miserable it was going to be.—
The misery at parting and my hatred of myself for caring so much. And at his callousness. He was so wise and Just. (C, 64–5)

Then the next day, as she says in her diary, she wondered how it had happened. "Why for the first time I have acted myself, and decided what to do of my own accord." (C, 65) What more important realization, and action than that? Never mind the misery and the misery to come, she had decided. And, as with all such decisions in general, there was no going back. Over and over in Carrington's life, she desired to unmake her first plan, to undo what she had undone, with Mark, with Gerald, with Lytton even. It is like Dorothy Bussy's running after her first letter to Gide to mail another: the imbalance of these situations seems to arouse such hesitations and repentings. And such drama.

Two of Carrington's portraits of Lytton typify her devotion. They are extraordinary in the sort of intimacy they show, with a sitter who is looking always at his book. One shows him reading in the garden at Tidmarsh, in 1918, in a deck chair, with the paper on the ground beside him, and his long fingers holding a book. (Lytton, in the great majority of his portraits, no matter who the painter, is reading. We could imagine André Gide in just such a position, reading to himself or aloud, idolized by Dorothy Bussy.) Beside Lytton on a small table reposes his panama hat with its dark band, and just behind him is a French window with its glass panes opening out into the garden where he sits reading, one thin leg crossed over the other, elegantly. The scene is calm.

But it is another portrait of him by Carrington that strikes me instantly. Lytton is stretched out full-length, his extremely long fingers holding his eternal book. He is portrayed as a sort of Byzantine saint, quiet, immortal, a figure made for worship. It is this painting that Frances Partridge had in her apartment and at which I stared for long periods, each time I went to see her, over so many long years. He seemed—how to say this?—like an icon of devotion, not just that of Carrington, whom Frances and I discussed at length, but of devotion itself. It reminded me of all the statues of *gisants* in cathedrals, those great dead marble people stretched out, sometimes with a dog at their feet.

This painting had been offered, at Carrington's death, to the National Portrait Gallery, which refused it. Was it that the painter was a woman, or some other reason? In any case, they now have it, as is only right, now that Frances is dead. Carrington loved this painting as she loved Lytton: it must have felt quite as present to her as he did. In her diary, on January 1, 1917 — which, in her distracted or careless state, because that is not what matters, she dates 1916 — she is talking, to herself and to Lytton:

> I wonder what you will think of it when you see it. I sit here, almost every night — it sometimes seems — looking at your picture, now tonight it looks wonderfully good, and I am happy. But then I dread showing it. I should like to go on always painting you every week, wasting the afternoon loitering, and never never showing you what I paint. It's marvellous having it all to oneself. No agony of the soul. Is it vanity? No, because I don't care for what they say. I hate only the indecency of showing them what I have loved. (C, 50)

The split between the intimate "you" and the others, the "them" that judge, is intense, as it will always be between "them" and the *us* that she and Lytton form. In the intimacy of that relation, marked as it is of course by the incapacity of lovemaking, about which Carrington has written extensively in her diary before, there is a kind of safety, of enclosedness.

The painting conveys all the wonder and terror of Carrington's adoration. How private it is: how it should not be shown to others. Here is the surprising part, until we try to understand it a bit: even not to the person loved. His portrait, with its so clear statement of adoration, is not always to be shared, in agony of soul, with the very person adored. The dread is double: showing it to others, but also showing it to the beloved. Intimacy does not require, in all cases, the sharing of the expression of emotion. Here is Carrington's profound instinctive comprehension of something indeed too deep for words. It is the image itself that reaches the profoundest depths. She has loved Lytton the way few people have the ability to love. Even during the rages of jealousy portrayed in the descriptions of her, alone, outside the lit windows of the house where Lytton is with his male lovers, and she sees them through the windowpanes, even during the loneliness and her own incapacities for painting, about which she always blames herself, it will be this relation of her mind and heart to the one she so terribly loves that will matter.

The long letter she writes on the night before her marriage to Ralph says it all, as movingly as any letter we could possibly imagine on such an occasion; taken with the painting, this diptych of emotion portrays Carrington as much as Lytton, when, at the crisis point, four years later than the painting, she has been living with Lytton at Tidmarsh and finally accepts Ralph's plea for marriage. This most extraordinary passage is worth dwelling upon for its style, its poignancy, and its drama. The plot is developed, stated, and we are witnesses, through her letter to Lytton, to the terribleness of it all. The very long letter, in three parts, begins as it is dated and timed: Saturday morning, 12 o'clock, May 14, 1921, and marked The Mill House, Tidmarsh. (How I love places, Carrington has said over and over. And this one she loves, even though from now on it will be marked with an awful sadness.) She has written many letters the night before, until three in the morning, and then worried about his showing them to others, or his leaving them about. This is the same worry we saw before about the painting and her wish not to show it to "them." For what she had with Lytton, always, was private.

Ralph has had a breakdown, has asked the Woolves what to do, and they have counseled either marriage or leaving Carrington. She had met him, he looked ill, and she worried, preferring to defer it, but, as she had said before to Lytton: "You see I knew there was nothing really to hope for from you—ever since the beginning." And now comes the terriblenesss: she had heard from Alix Strachey that Lytton had told her husband, James, that he was terrified of her clinging on to him like "a permanent limpet and other things." (C, 175). This is the background of her Tidmarsh letter.

Carrington always had an acute sense of place. It was at the foot of the Swindon Downs, just outside Chiseldon, that Ralph had told her what Lytton had said, no doubt the same sort of thing that Alix recounted. She had as she writes to Lytton, become terrified of "being physically on your nerves and revolting you. I never came again to your bedroom . . . all these years I have known all along that my life with you was limited. I could never hope for it to become permanent. After all, Lytton, you are the only person who I have ever had an all absorbing passion for. I shall never have another. I couldn't now. I had one of the most self abasing loves that a person can have."

But, she goes on, these years at Tidmarsh have been the happiest she has ever spent, and they will always be friends, and he will be relieved at Ralph taking her away, "so to speak, off your hands." She is aware, she says, of the "moment I am getting on your nerves and when I am not wanted."

> Still it's too much of a strain to be quite alone here waiting to see you or craning my nose and eyes out of the top window at 41 Gordon Square to see if you are coming down the street, when I know we'll be better friends, if you aren't haunted by the idea that I am sitting depressed in some corner of the world waiting for your footstep. (C, 176)

It won't make much difference, she says, and it will make Ralph so happy. Here is the most awful part, and it relates to Virginia and Leonard. It is again about the others and their judgment of her, as Ralph related it, in bed, of all places:

> Last night in bed he told me everything Virginia and Leonard had told him. Again a conversation you had with them was repeated to me. Ralph was so happy he didn't hear me gasp and as it was dark he didn't see the tears run down my cheeks. Virginia told him that you had told them you didn't intend to come to Tidmarsh much after Italy and you were nervous lest I'd feel I had a sort of claim on you if I lived with [you] for a long time, ten years, and that they all wondered how you could have stood me so long and how on earth we lived together alone here, as I didn't understand a word of literature and we had nothing in common intellectually or physically. That was wrong. For nobody I think could have loved the Ballades, Donne, and Macaulay's Essays and best of all, Lytton's Essays as much as I. . . . So now I shall never tell *you* I do care again. It goes after today somewhere deep down inside me and I'll not resurrect it to hurt either you, or Ralph. Never again. (C, 176)

Ralph, even knowing she could not really love him, content with his fate, happily returned to sleep, while she lay there weeping over the

> savage cynical fate which had made it impossible for my love ever to be used by you. You never knew, or never will know the very big and devastating love I had for you. How I adored every hair, every curl on your beard. How I devoured you whilst you read to me at night. How I loved the smell of your face in the sponge. Then the ivory skin on your hands, your voice, and your hat when I saw it coming along the top of the garden wall from my window. Say you will remember it, that it wasn't all lost and that you'll forgive me for this outburst, and always be my friend. . . . (C, 176)

And then later, at 3 in the afternoon, saying he had given her a much longer life than she had deserved:

> You who I would have given the world to have made happier than any person could be. . . . I'll always care as much, only now it will never burden you and we'll never discuss it again. . . . But I keep on crying, if I stop and think about you. Outside the sun is baking and they all chatter, and laugh. It's cynical, this world in its opposites. Once you said to me, that Wednesday afternoon in the sitting room, you loved me as a friend. Could you tell it to me again? (C, 178).

This letter, unforgettable in all its parts, is a refusal to repress her love, and an acceptance of the awfulness of what it must comport. Her marriage, a sort of ultimate sacrifice, is what she can give, and does.

What she gave was a lot, and connected her unsureness about her painting with her personal problems. On March 14, 1922, she writes to Gerald: "Why do I never tell you of my painting, because I am often sad about it, and I think & think & draw picture after picture & then so little is ever painted." And this discouragement ties up with her frequent sadness over Lytton: "I have loved Lytton for 6 years. He might have had my love for the rest of his life if he wanted it. He might have made me his boot-black, or taken me to Siberia and I would have given up every friend I had to be with him . . . and now it's all gone melted down & smothered with pillow after pillow of despair, and finally put away in an envelope the day I married Ralph—and Ralph can make me care for him in every way except the way he wants me." (HRRC)

The ups and downs in her artistic life are as intense as in her personal life. Sometimes it seems hopeful. On August 15 of 1921, she writes Gerald from Watendlath Farm, near Keswick, in Cumberland, where she and Lytton are staying with a Mrs. Wilson. They have returned from Windemere, and she is exulting in the landscape. "The grass is a most lucious green & so soft to the feet, and crunchy." She writes of their long walks, and of the heather smell of honey, so strong she longs to put it on brown bread—all she can think of. Except drawing, and that because her easel has not yet come. "The evening was still so lovely, that I sat & drew a white cottage & a Barn with a arrangement of trees & hills, sitting on a little hill until it grew too cold. Really this is an astounding place for pictures. The trees are so marvelous solid, like trees in some old Titian picture, & the houses such wonderful greys, & whites, and then the formation of the hills so varied.

I think very hard whilst I moon about on the hills, arrangements for my pictures." (HRRC)

But then the feeling falls apart. She writes to Gerald on October 12, 1921, plunged in discouragement: "I think it's terribly depressing looking at one's past work. I intend to paint out every single canvas & burn all the drawings tomorrow." She had intended a large painting, but is exhausted, energyless—and vacant. "I have not started my life yet." (HRRC)

When Lytton dies, and she has failed to put an end to herself by asphyxiation in the garage, thinking this might permit him to live— some exchange she had hoped for, in her all-loving and superstitious way—she is bereft in a particularly acute way. Carrington's sense of the visual is all the more terrible here. Lytton's face looks like "the Goya painting of a dead man with the high light on the cheek bones." (481) After her attempt at suicide has failed, after she had hoped so hard that her death might bring Lytton back to life, after she stands there listening to the blackbird singing outside in the sun on the aspen tree, time having "lost all its properties," she places the bay leaves Ralph has brought her, that she has made into a wreath, too large for her head, on Lytton's head as he lies there dead: "the olive green leaves against his ivory skin. I kissed his eyes, and his ice cold lips. The sun shone through the open window. . . . It is ironical that Lytton by that early attack at 6 oclock saved my life. When I gave my life for his, he should give it back."

Her bereft self will not be long living:

Diary Feb. 11 (1932)
No one will ever know the special perfectness of Lytton. . . . For every mood of his instantly made me feel in the same mood. All gone. And I never told him or showed him how utterly I loved him. . . . What point is there now in what I see every day, in conversations, jokes, beautiful visions, pains, even nightmares? . . . I just feel I must get through these days, and pray they won't be very many more. (C, 484)

She remembered Lytton reading to her David Hume's 1777 essay on suicide. "And we both agreed on the sense and truth of the arguments." But she has been told by her friends that it isn't a good time to decide things so soon after the shock. So

I will defer my decision for a month or two until the result of the operation is less acute. . . . Really I have decided and if I bring myself to think of reality for a few hours how could I bear the emptiness and loneliness of life without Lytton? no one will ever know the utter happiness of our life together.

Feb. 12th, Diary (1932)
If I could sit here alone just holding his clothes in my arms on the sofa with that handkerchief over my face I feel I would get comfort, but I know these feelings are bad. . . . So I must and cannot go backwards to his grave. . . . Oh Lytton darling, you are dead. . . . And all is utterly cold and grey on this early morn. . . . All your books in the library that we loved together so fondly and arranged evening after evening. They are desolate. . . . Your brown writing case that I bought you in Aix. Your clothes that I chose with you at Carpentier and Packer. . . . I see my paints and think it is no use, for Lytton will never see my pictures now, and I cry. (C, 494)

She will never see anything of what she loves again. In her diary from February 16, 1932: "Just a few book plates in some books and never again, however long I look out of the window, will I see your tall thin figure walking across the park past the dwarf pine past the stumps." (C, 494)

She found life not worth living once he was dead and his things burned, his glasses atop the heap of them all, except his coats and ties that she would give to his friends like talismans. The last friend Carrington was to see was Virginia Woolf, into whose arms she flung herself. It was her letter that she received right before pulling the trigger of the shotgun, which was misaimed, so that she shot off half her side before she was finally able to die.

Her relation to Virginia had been intensely complicated. In 1916, when she first knew her, she used to fear seeing her alone, writing to Lytton on December 8, 1916: "Dinner tonight with Virginia tout seul. Pray for me." But at other times, as on September 25, 1923, she would state her overwhelming affection for her. Virginia was always fascinating to Carrington: "I like the Woolves far more than they like me. Ugh. I have a queer love for Virginia which fills me with emotion when I see her. They talk better than any people I know. How quickly the conversation becomes intelligent and amusing when Virginia talks!" (C, 261)

Virginia was fascinated by her, this curious person dressed in her little short jackets and skirts, strange and funny. Carrington had written Virginia, after Lytton's death, in February, that she was the first person Carrington would like to see in London when she came up, and when

Virginia came to see Carrington and begged her to come to London, Carrington said she "would or not." Perhaps she did not then know whether, indeed, she would or not. We have no way of knowing what she knew.

But Virginia's diary is haunted for a long time by one thought: "Oh but Carrington," she had written, in the note that Carrington received the day she died, "we have to live and be ourselves." But Carrington could not, or would not, in any case did not want to live. This is part of the story that requires different interpretations. Alas, says David Garnett, why could she not have taken pride in her work? Why did she have to die of love?

She also died of her own intensity, I feel. And, given the writings and paintings she left us, particularly that portrait of her beloved Lytton stretched out full length like a Byzantine saint with his book, given her sense of the visual and of the excruciating high and low points of life, I think she could have done nothing else. I feel strongly that we should salute, again, that truly extraordinary possibility she manifested of an unselfish love. How incongruous, said Mark Gertler, just as Dorothy Bussy spoke of the incongruous nature of the relation she and Gide bore to each other. Incongruous, this refusal of the ordinary acceptance of things as they are seen to be, "normally." But, in a sense, these relations worked, and enabled the best work of the women who so loved. I do not see that we can ask anything more.

Chapter 7

Claude Cahun

Island of Courage

I would like not to sew, pierce, kill with anything but the extreme point. . . . Never to voyage except at the prow of myself.

—*(E, 115)*

Not to define herself; this was her ambition from the beginning. Born in Nantes in 1894, Lucie Renée Mathilde Schwob would later call herself Lucy, so as in no way to adopt anything her mother had given her, even those two letters for the ending of her name, "ie." When her mother was repeatedly interned in a clinic for psychopathological problems, Lucy lived in Nantes with her paternal grandmother. There at school, she was intimidated by her anti-Semitic classmates, withdrawn from the school, and sent to England to study. She was completely bilingual, like Emily Carr; and these so different women wrote in both languages, interchangeably.

In 1909 Lucy Schwob returned to school in Nantes, and fell in love with Suzanne Malherbe, two years younger. Their families were friends, and upon the death of Lucy's mother, her father, Maurice Schwob, married Suzanne's mother. From now on, Lucy and Suzanne, stepsisters and lovers, would live together, first in a room above the journal *Le Phare de la Loire*, run by Lucy's father; then on the Rue de Grenelle in Paris; then at 70 bis, rue Notre-Dame-des-Champs, near Montparnasse; and finally in La Roquaise at St. Brelade's Bay, on the Island of Jersey.

Now calling herself Claude Courlis ("anteater," presumably in honor of the long nose of Marcel Schwob, her writer uncle)— "Claude" chosen as a deliberately androgynous name and Schwob rejected perhaps because of her early bouts with anti-Semitism—she spent her nights reading in the bookshop of Maurice's journal. In that publication, she would soon publish a chronicle of fashion, under the guise of a man, in the opposite mode from Stephane Mallarme's publication of *La Dernière Mode*, of 1872, in which he wrote the majority of articles in the guise of several women: Mademoiselle X, Mme de Ponty, and so on. Here she is, in 1914, writing in this fashion—actually it does not sound so unlike Mallarmé the fashion writer:

> This winter, transformed by the Oriental model, the veil is returning, more elegant than ever. Now it is called "mooresque": thicker on the bottom of the face, it only lets your eyes appear.
> —Take care of them. [your eyes]
> Mother-Grand, we are putting a beauty spot of black velvet on a diaphanous veil: what do you think of that? (E, 439)

Suzanne would take the name of Moore, equally androgynous. Claude published *Vues et Visions* in *Le Mercure de France* in 1914, became anorexic, and made several suicide attempts. Always she felt herself fatally pre-condemned: "Before I was born, I was condemned. Sentenced in absentia." (E, 19) Indeed, during the entire length of her life, there seems to have been little joy or spontaneity. Her calculated self-portraiture traces the history of a brilliantly performed narcissistic self-consciousness, at the extreme point of what Antonin Artaud called a Theatre of Cruelty—which he defined as extreme will. Nothing is lost in sentimental squishiness, no words simply thrown away. One of the most remarkable characteristics of Lucy Schwob's writing is its unforgiving pointedness—it neither describes nor analyzes emotions. It simply—or rather, complicatedly—depicts, always herself, in multiple.

By 1916 she would be calling herself Claude Cahun—and sometimes, Daniel Douglas, in mocking counterpart to Oscar Wilde's nemesis Alfred Douglas. She had written about the Wilde trial, and, as a lesbian, was particularly angry with the unjust outcome. She wrote also about Wilde's play *Salomé*—banned in puritanical England—with the French publication of which Pierre Louys and Marcel Schwob, her uncle, concerned themselves, and in which Sarah Bernhardt performed in 1893.

Claude herself would work in the theatre Le Plateau, run by Pierre Albert-Birot, and photographs of her in her roles, especially in *Bluebeard*, abound. She was a consummate performer in all senses, as an actress/actor and as an actor/actress of the many self-disguises she chose: in roles from sailor to boxer to vamp to the pilot Amelia Earhart. She would spend much of her life putting herself on the stage in photography—that is, *La mise-en-scène de soi*. These polymorphous portraits, in which she plays many roles, are echoed by her writings, particularly *Heroines*, in which Helen, Judith, and others take leading parts.

Helen is, like all the others, a masterpiece of irony:

Helen the Rebel

I know perfectly well that I'm ugly, but I try to forget it. I act beautifully. In everything and especially when the enemy is around, *I act absolutely as if I were most beautiful. It's the secret of my charm.* What a lie! And I'll end up by believing it. When Menelaus married me I was young, and unknown, despite my birth. But I love him. He is so blond! Already by instinct, feminine instinct, I played my role of goddess for him (daughter of Jupiter and Leda—no, not Leda, Venus. Venus wanted to have some swan too.) I dazzled him. The arrows of my tender brother put out his eyes. I swore never to belong to any mortal on this earth: Helen is reserved for the bed of the gods. In short, I put my value way up, and knew how to put such a high price on possessing me that he never thought about bargaining.

. . .

Agamemnon was my first lover.—Excellent bait to attract the others.—Aside from that, a middling success. I really think he only took me out of consideration for his brother. He couldn't resist teasing— holding my chin lifted towards himself, the greatest of men: "It's not that you are really pretty, pretty . . . but ok! Luckily, it all happened in the family!

These writings are quite as extraordinary as her photographs, and in both instances, bear out the ambition to make the self of everything available: " 'le moi se fait de tout." As Eve Sedgwick and others have pointed out, the construction of the self through multiple guises is comparable to a sort of deconstruction of identity—this is as true of the verbal as of the visual. Even the farm on which Suzanne and Claude would eventually live on the Island of Jersey would be called "The Farm without a Name" (*La ferme sans nom*), and in her resistance work, Claude would call herself "the Soldier without a name." So much for the given name and the adopted name.

Of course, the androgynous and the bisexual roles call upon various parts of the personality, and Cahun, in her various guises and names, called upon much that was unusual in the 1920s and 1930s. This period of her life has been examined repeatedly by many current commentators in queer and lesbian publications—the bibliography is long and growing longer every day. It is both ironic and flavorful that this tendency of self-portraiture as the other should be termed Bovaryism, defined as conceiving yourself as other than what or who you are. Emma Bovary, projecting herself into the roles she read, endures as icon, metaphor, and heroine of otherness: about her, "*c'est moi,*" said Flaubert, and, on another occasion, "*ce n'est pas moi.*" That is exactly the point: being who you aren't—Bovaryism, Cahunism, Cindy Shermanism. That Cahun reflected at such length on narcissism speaks already of her intense self-consciousness, never a problem if you are to be a subject of contemporary commentary.

In 1925, Claude sent some of her dream narratives to Belgium's *Le Disque vert*, run by Jacques Viot and Henri Michaux, who were enthusiastic about them. Michaux wrote to her about her narratives, of which she had sent him only samples, remarking on the "independence" of the pages. This might lead us to speculate on exactly what they are independent of: her uncle? society's point of view? She was always clearly rebellious, and when we read these dreams he wanted to publish, and did, her detestation of polite notions of family is ultra-clear. "If your dreams are like that . . . and you put them on paper, I would be glorious for publishing them." He was, of course, famous for much else he published, as was she—but all the same, the initial contact through this violent expression of nonconformism was to prove important. Michaux visited the couple often in Jersey, and was designated by Claude, were Suzanne to die before her, as the administrator of her estate.

Here are Claude's dreams, as she wrote them in 1924, and as they were published in *Le Disque vert* of 1925:

Dream Tales

I willingly recognize all my thoughts, even those whose authorship might be a bit dubious. My desires, if they can't be realized in real life, spread out—or then harden and lengthen into waking dreams. Lacking both scruples and remorse, my memory is bad and only retains from sleep the temperature, the agreeable contact. So does the sea caress our body and slip between our fingers. Life infinitely divisible, corals, little snake slipping by . . . If by some chance I am holding the tail of the lazy lizard, I pull at it; it breaks off. I cast it away, while walking through the field of clubs, anyone more superstitious than me might think even now that two and one make four, and still believe in its value! I nevertheless consent to the dreams that follow: To attribute them to me will make them particularly plausible, even to me.

(Childhood)
I

My *mother* (if I name the feminine first, it isn't to make it more important—everything is equal to me—but very French gallantry). My mother caresses me with one hand and beats my father with the other.

2

My father holds me on his knees. He has just lit a footwarmer in the shape of a fullsize coffin, and I see it contains my mother slowly burning alive . . .

3

I snatch at the moustaches of my father which stretch out until they become reins I am holding very tight, while in one corner my mother is sitting impaled on an iron candle spike, and lighting herself, *a living torch* . . .

(*Puberty*)
4

The river bed is drying up . . .
My parents are making love tenderly, differently, abusively, confusedly, then simply, and again tenderly . . .
I watch them doing it.

5

A slug is swallowing a snake that is swallowing it right back. Soon there are left only the tails or the jaws. (I can't remember by which end it started).

(*Grownup Nights*)
6

Thursday nights, I am dreaming about Robinson Crusoe whom I conceive in my own image. An Island, isolation! Someone has set a date with me in the ivory tower. It's me. I rush so as not to keep myself wait-ing. Then, taking myself as a center, plunging in my heart one hand of the compass, I busy myself with tracing ditches, digging, less romanti-cally, some channels across the road; I grow roses because of the thorns; I cultivate brambles and the bottoms of bottles. Let no ship get near my port, even should it raise a European flag or a Global one! I would shipwreck it.

7

I have a horror of my empty room. My friends are late. I go from the open door to the window and lean outside: a thousand couples are walking towards my house. I laugh joyously. Then I weep: it will be too small. But the walls spread out magically. Sandwiches, petits-fours, and carafes multiply. My heart swells enormously. There will be enough for everyone.

8

The whiteness of the rough sheet. Smell of lilies. How my dark body is desirable! — Is it dark? Is it my body? — A splotch of sperm in admirable shaper.

(Old Age)
9

The sea pounds against the soft rocks. It gets stuck. My nose is freez-ing and thinning out; my flesh is falling away. Soon there will be only a marrow bone sucked in greedily by the wind.

("About Dreams," E, 483–4)

The over-the-top violence against the hated mother, and the erotic force of the dreams, are supreme examples of the voyage at the edge, at the very tip of the self that Claude Cahun chose for her self-representation in writing as well as in photography.

Surrealist writing, we might say of her work. And Claude Cahun was treated as part of the surrealist circle around André Breton, for whom she always felt a kind of passion. But, sadly, her spectacular eccentrici-ties were not such as to appeal to him, as Jacqueline Lamba, his wife, pointed out. Spectacularly inappropriate was this affection of Claude's—but perhaps that was the point. As with Nadja, the mad-woman he had loved and then left, because she was boring him with her madness (today she was just reading the menu of the restaurant aloud, he said upon one occasion), Claude was displeasing in her very unconformity; in 1920 and again in 1929, she shaved her head bald, often dying her scalp gold or pink or green, not the type of beauty Breton would choose. His relatively conformist personality, despite his unconformist theories and longings, made him turn away precisely from the demonstrations that might have seemed in complete accordance with his views. Claude had always loved him in a way "more impossible, more secret, more desperately mad than all her real or fictional loves." (E, 143)

He might have been in awe of a certain conception of madness—the art of madmen and children yields, as he said, "the key to the fields." But when it was a question of everyday behavior, it was something else. One day a flag passed in the street—a symbol of French patriotism—and Nadja insulted it. She could, he said, simply have turned away. This is in odd disaccord with the celebrated photograph of Breton's most faithful surrealist adept, Benjamin Péret, the celebrated photograph of him spitting at a priest. When Nadja, in the story that bears her name, tried to put her hand over Breton's and her own eyes, as he was driving, that was the limit. He turned to someone less mad, as he himself writes, and then "they came to tell him that Nadja was in an asylum." There is, in the text, a long empty space in front of this announcement by the others, as if—from my reader's point of view—his distance from the madwoman were already marking itself. Mad women were not Breton's choice, clearly. And he would give up his favorite cafe if Suzanne and Claude were sitting there, with their odd comportment and appearance. Dressed as a man with a monocle, or then, her face plastered over with expressionist makeup, Claude felt, in her dandy outfits, close to Salvador Dali "Salvador Dollars," once he had been successfully removed from the Surrealist group) in his outrageous clothing and appearance—green suit, massive moustaches curling around his mouth, accompanied by Gala with her expressionless gray face and stiffly curled hair. Dandies, all of them.

Nevertheless, Jacqueline Lamba, Breton's wife, remained close to Claude, whose photographic portraits of the Bretons—some in front of a curtain, staging them as she staged herself—remain unequalled. As do her portraits of her lifelong friends Henri Michaux and Robert Desnos. Her famous photograph of Jacqueline leaning on a window is variously imagined as being taken on the Island of Jersey in 1939 when she and her daughter Aube were visiting Claude and Suzanne in their farm there, or, by other viewers, as being taken when Jacqueline was pregnant with Aube. It is in either case a superb picturing of Jacqueline in an unusually tender moment.

Part of the surrealist program was—if somewhat less visibly demonstrative than Péret's spitting at priests—an attack against the religious practices and beliefs of the church, whatever its mode or denomination. Asked to write for a 1926 number of the journal *Philosophies*, on the topic of God (what are your thoughts about this?), Claude answered at some length, in 1925, approximately a year after writing the dream texts. An excerpt gives the flavor of her reflection:

(Tell us about some thought you might have on the theme: God)
Meditation of Mlle Lucie Schwob
. . . You see your angel, never someone else's angel, I think.
—Rimbaud

I can answer your question only in a way you will probably find very silly, very feminine. But perhaps I will be excused because this answer will be frank, revealing, just as you would like it to be, and so will serve as an opposite pole for your own god, who will seem to you all the more *worthy of adoration*, as mine will seem *grotesque* to you.

God is for me

1. MAN—Prince Charming, indivisible in dreams, scattered all about in the real world, and so deceiving me with approximations, god eminently variable in his thousand incarnations—all imperfect, relative. . . . My Prince Charming is none other than God the Father.

2. SUPERMAN—The Messiah, he who possesses the philosopher's stone of virtues, who can make gold with the lead of souls. He can only be my son (my *gold* is the only true one—all your values are false), and since I am sterile, I am equally sceptical: I don't believe in the police raid of an all-powerful Messiah . . . Eternally disincarnated, for as soon as he is born it's in a prison of nerves and bone, I nevertheless conceive and adore God the *Son*.

3. ME—Not as I am, obviously, but the way I should be—that I would like to be, if you prefer. Bovaryism. A god as fleeting, as disincarnated as the two others. This soul often plays hooky. It even escapes its best master: pride. . . . Never mind, it's a god , and the nearest, the most malleable: the *Holy Spirit*.

TRINITY—The dissociation I make is artificial. No matter which of the three members is always ready, its mouth open, to devour others, to assimilate the world to itself. The most inanimate objects, through symbolic strength, often take hold of lightning, and pretend to be God. A relation that is only love, and the most terrestrial form, must have some fetishism to it. You have the god you deserve. Too bad.

We always find the word GOD lovely, adorable, as long as it is ours. It's the gods of others we find grotesque, or just funny—depending on whether we are serious or light in temperament.

. . .

The word GOD is necessary—because it is.
It's perhaps the word that has the most meaning. Which makes you wonder if it has any. (E, 480)

In 1930 appeared her most famous publication, *Aveux non avenus* (Unconfessed or Absent Confessions), illustrating the stripping down of the self at its most extreme point. It is a self-portrait with a vengeance, and now the vengeance that was once turned against the family, specifically the mother, as manifested in the dreams, is turned against the self. This time, it feels drastic, undreamed, real:

There is too much of everything. And I am silent. I hold my breath. I lie down inside a circle, I withdraw from my edges, I fold myself into an imaginary center. . . . I have my hair shaved off, my teeth extracted, and my breasts—everything that bothers or blocks my gaze— stomach, ovaries, brain, clotted and conscious. When I notice nothing but a heartbeat, perfected, I will of course have won. (E, 110)

Performing the crucial and the cruel, Claude becomes at once mask and nudity, theatre and audience. Antonin Artaud's Theatre of Cruelty has found its perfect expression in this declaration—necessity in will, the stripping down of ordinary language for the bare gesture. Her uncle Marcel Schwob, whom Claude resembles—see her self-portrait in exactly his pose and profile—shaved his head until it bled, and quoted, as she did, Baudelaire: "the beautiful is always bizarre." (E, 115) In the superb and superlative majesty of artificial forms, Claude Cahun reached the limit with her famous portrait with the ovoid skull, deformed like the surrealist photographs of Andre Kertesz—as far from the natural as one could possibly get.

Interior exoticism, it has been called, and that seems to me just right. Anyone who wants to travel not outside the self, but at the very prow of the stripped-down self, risks incomprehension from others and frequently, inescapably, a disregard for the self. Claude felt damned before she was born, as in the already quoted passage: "Before I was born, I was condemned. Sentenced in absentia." (E, 19)

Always admitting her monstrous egoism, she hated and loved herself. Her intense contradictions in her personal psychology rendered her participation both visible and problematic: "I write against myself," she would say: "J'écris contre moi." (E, 538) No wonder she was obsessed by the figure of Narcissus.

The writing in *Unconfessed Confessions* (published as *Aveux Non Avenus*, Ed. du Carrefour, May 30, 1930) has a particular flavor to it. (The name of the publisher—carrefour or crossroads—has its own flavor of cross-gendering, so it is especially appropriate.) The writing is hermetic, complicated, ultimately as infolded on itself as the illustrations and the photographs accompanying it. The "invisible adventure," it is called on the first page, and its difficulty obscures its sense. The reader is lured in precisely by the feeling of almost understanding—which is then cut off. It is hard writing—the exact opposite from the kind of text Claude will leave behind after the war, when she has been through so much else, so differently. Here she is still at the crossroads of identifying herself as a lesbian revolutionary—self-involved. A photographer and a narcissist:

> The photographer's lens follows the eyes, the mouth, the wrinkles on the skin. . . . The expression of the face is violent, tragic at times. Finally calm—a calm conscience, that of acrobats, so elaborate. A professional smile—and there you are.
>
> The pocket mirror reappears, the rouge and the powder around the eyes. A little pause. A period. Paragraph.
> I start over.
> . . .
> But what a ridiculous circus for those who haven't seen—and I haven't shown anything—the obstacles, the abysses, and the steps taken.
> . . .
> While waiting to see clearly, I want to hunt myself down, to struggle. Who, feeling armed against himself, even with truely useless words, who would not try, even if it were just placing the full into the void?
> It's false. It's not a lot. But it gives the eye some practice.
> . . .
> Here's a part called Myself (for want of anything better.)
> The mermaid succumbs to her own voice.
>
> Narcissus: it seemed to me the most incomprehensible thing. Only one explanation is possible: Narcissus didn't love himself. He let himself be deceived by an image. He didn't know how to traverse appearances. If he had loved a nymph's face instead of his own, his deadly impotence would have stayed the same.

But if he had been able to love himself through his mirage, his good fortune would have been worthy of the envy of all the ages, the symbol of a living paradise, the myth of a privileged man.

. . .

Oh Narcissus, you could have loved yourself in every way: the sun, your brother, lovelier in the tired night, who looked over the moon at a pallor he never tired of admiring. . . .
You could have loved yourself among the nymphs . . . you could have isolated yourself from the universe.

. . .

Self-love. A hand tensed on a mirror—a mouth, quivering nostrils— between swooning eyelids, the mad fixity of enlarged pupils. . . .

. . .

Finally, what most bothers Narcissus the voyeur is the insufficiency, the discontinuity of his own gaze.

. . .

Why does God force me to change faces? Why does he upset my painful virtues? . . .

. . .

I can't answer my own questions. Perhaps another time I will spread out my nets better.

The change of face, forced by God or herself, was part of the will to androgny. As she says in the middle of the text: "Masculine? Feminine? But that depends on the case. Neuter is the only gender which always suits me. If it existed in our language you wouldn't see me floating around in my thought. I would be forever the worker bee." (quoted in Murat, 392) In Paris, Claude belonged to the Association des Ecrivains et Artistes Révolutionnaires in 1932, signed the surrealist declarations of 1933, and the Contr'attaque Manifesto and worked with that group, headed by Georges Bataille, from June 33 to October 35. She was never politically uninvolved.

By 1936, Claude was exhibiting her objects—surrealist objects, if there ever were any—at the Charles Ratton gallery. These were deeply "irrational objects," unuseful, and downright scary. They mixed heterogenous elements to the point of dizziness, with things stuck on, out, to the side, quite like some of her photographic experiments that mingle fragments of bodies in a helter-skelter sort of rhythm: hands, feet, magnifying glasses, eyes, pieces of this and that, as of these and those. We see Moore's face and then Claude's face, hands of one and of the other. As is always the case in Claude's world, nothing is simple, everything is mingled in a deliberate and fearful confusion, mangling as well as mingling.

During the occupation of the island of Jersey by the Germans, Suzanne and Claude were active in the resistance. On St. Brelade Bay, the two women would bathe naked, and distribute anti-Nazi pamphlets, taking risks at every moment. They placed in full sight banners reading, in the German in which Suzanne was proficient, such slogans as: "Jesus is big—But Hitler is bigger. And so Jesus Died for Men.—But Men die for Hitler." They painted crosses black and planted them in the cemetery, marking them: "The war is over for you . . ." They stuck butterflies on German tanks.

In March of 1944, Claude was called to the Kommandatur under the name Lucy Schwob. With a shawl over her head and this name that was not threatening, she seemed not part of the resistance. As Claude writes of this time, "They made excuses to the old lady in black who seemed so sick they were persuaded we couldn't be more than accomplices." (E, 281) They worked on. However, Claude had to buy cartons of cigarette paper to wrap tracts in, and the seller informed on them. It was almost too late, for Germany by this point had lost the war. Arrested again, she was this time accused, when one of the tracts was found in her bag, of "Insults to the Fuhrer, to the Grand Reich, to the army." They were both imprisoned and condemned to death. They had decided to kill themselves in their cells, and were preparing to take heavy doses of Gardenal, after they were judged guilty, and sentenced to death. Fortunately, the date of their execution was delayed, to February 20, 1945, and the island of Jersey was liberated on May 8 of 1944.

In 1948–49 Claude had started to assemble her notes on the resistance, under the title *Le Muet dans la Melée/Silent in the Struggle*. (E, 181) Nothing more accurately told what she saw as the Poetic Truth, *la vérité poétique*. "C'est par la force des images que par la suite des temps, pourraient bien s'accomplir les vraies révolutions." She wrote, quoting St.-Pol Roux, the Breton poet who was a victim of the Nazis: "It's by the strength of images that, as time goes on, true revolutions can be brought about." The scrapbook she had begun contained the fragments of a tale about the occupation in Jersey, and how she and Suzanne dealt with it. I dressed, she wrote, "like everyone else: no hat, old jodphurs, Wellingtons, a wool jersey, a semi-masculine jacket, a Burberry with lots of pockets for tracts, a scarf around my head, in loud colors, wool gloves, and a market bag." I was Lucy Schwob, she said, and I looked like an old sick lady. (E, 627)

She kept a French diary in code, and launched, here and there, champagne bottles with texts about the success of the Resistance in

France. Often they would leave indecipherable messages, and "to keep the German police out of mischief" they would invent meetings in German. Their tracts would be signed "The Solder without a name" (*der Soldat ohne Namen*), and were often written in the Czech language, of which they had a very imperfect knowledge. But of course that was to throw the Germans off the scent of these two French women. They would pin pamphlets on cars, about how Germany was losing the war, and so on.

The texts were put into German by Suzanne: "The Gestapo are carousing and not defending the Fatherland. They are afraid, are even afraid of their shadow. . . . Solders without a name, all against these cowards, these gluttons, these stool pigeons. . . . ! The end of the war is near." They lived as best they could, picking up cigar butts in the street and drying them before using them. Suzanne would smoke a pipe, Claude would make cigarettes.

When they were imprisoned, they were in separate cells, isolated, but Claude would stick out her arm through her peephole to have Suzanne recognize it. A harmonica was passed from cell to cell so that the prisoners could cheer each other up. And then one day, Claude wrote, "I remembered the 26 of August when I saw through my peephole Suzanne's hand open in a V meaning the liberation of Paris. . . ." (E, 634–46)

Claude reflected, after it was all over, on what had pulled her through.

> I couldn't have endured it without the struggle that gave me indirectly and a hundredfold the relations which I suffered from not having directly. And moreover, despite the immediate presence, never wavering, of my nearest love, without the other: the one that has no sex and no country, I would have died from hatred. Despite dreams, the towers raised in the night, the bridges cast towards the shining shores, the tidal waves of mirages submerging all reality, its ebb and flow, the crumbling of the towers and bridges and their resurrection, this perpetual, this captivating prodigy, without the other dream: that you have to share immediately with no matter whom, I would have died from avarice . . .

Unlike Suzanne, Claude found herself indulging in impoliteness, rendering herself ridiculous, she thought, whereas Suzanne would smile "at the avid ones and their treason. Never were we so far from each other." "No," said Claude far more severe than her lover,

> I can't admit these flowers of forgetting, these model fruits, these opportunistic greetings, these bouquets of artifices . . .

If ever a reader holds out his hand to me, it could only be a proud hand. He knows me a rebel, asocial—a revolutionary dreamer. . . . who doesn't agree with any political party. Without any position in the world, without an exceptional talent and without any hidden power. But if I accept a hand held out, is it with the candor I would have put in it formerly. To resist the temptation of leaning on someone else, putting in someone else the absolute confidence I can't give myself without anguish, that's what I needed, what I still have to learn.

There is the human condition. I had been well placed to observe it from inside, from outside and from close up, under diverse angles, to sense what it would be like across Europe, what it would impose and permit its imposition on itself. (664–5)

Suzanne and Claude were awarded the Silver Medal of la Reconnaissance Française in January of 1951. Let me venture to say in answer to what Claude once called her "morbid obsession; what can I do?" ("Cette obsession morbide: que puis-je?) that Claude Cahun did an amazing amount. She was lover and actor, writer and photographer, revolutionary and always a performer at the extreme point of herself, just as she would have hoped.

At the end of her life, Claude was still longing to return to Paris, to be part of the surrealists gathered there. But she couldn't leave her three cats: the brown one, the blonde one, and the Blue Persian, her companion for eight years. A photograph shows her face enveloped in a shawl, as she walks along Le Chemin des Chats—their favorite and hers.

In 1953, she stayed in the Hôtel Le Royal, and then in the Lutetia, and tried to find an apartment. She would go to the Cafe de la Mairie, where Contre'attaque met, and there met up with Breton and other surrealists: Benjamin Peret, Méret Oppenheim, and the painter Marie Cerminova, known as Toyen. But, weakened by the harsh imprisonment, she returned to the island of Jersey, ill. She never recuperated from her illnesses, affecting her eyes and lungs and kidneys. Shortly before her death, she wrote André Breton, for whom she had always an enormous affection: "I dangerously upset my mind for those I love. Warning; you are among them."

She died in the hospital in Jersey, of a heart attack, on December 8, 1954.

CONCLUSION

RESISTANCE AND REFUSAL

Arthur Rimbaud fulminated, at the end of the nineteenth century, against "les assis," or the seated comfortable bourgeois types—they were well-off, and their behavior was always appropriate to their situation, in which they were at ease. I have defined my notion of the eccentric as exactly the opposite: qualified by a comportment that would generally be deemed inappropriate to the circumstances of the life as received. Against the givens of each situation—set by social or traditional norms— these seven women made distinctly unusual choices, rejecting a behavior that would have been thought rational, choosing, rather, the irrational, the unexpected. They dressed in ways suited to their way of thinking and living, as opposed to ordinary *bienséance*. Judith's flowing Oriental robes, Paula's flower or amber necklace, Dorothy's little white lace collar, Suzanne Valadon and Emily Carr appearing at their exhibitions in remarkably unbecoming garments—a gunnysack, a headband, flat shoes and socks, with raucous laughs: all these were the very opposite of a Marie Laurencin with her perfectly chosen garments. Carrington wore her little vests and turned her toes in, and Claude Cahun shaved off her hair and dyed her scalp pink, gold, or green. Each, rebellious in her fashion, resisted what would have been easier than the form of life she chose. Each refusal of rational comportment contributed to the intensity of feeling, which nourished the work.

Every tale has a center. Sometimes it reveals itself in relation to another person, sometimes in relation to a creative work, or a place, or an event. This can be a crisis point or then a continuing intensifying element. So we might see Judith Gautier's Orientalist character as defining her, as much as her relations to Hugo and Wagner, and the wildly bohemian and antisocial nature of Suzanne Valadon as her center, from beginning to end Paula Modersohn-Becker's passionate relation to her work made her rebellious against her heritage and her marriage, and earned her Rilke's epic salute. Dorothy Bussy's passionate relation to André Gide and Carrington's to Dorothy's brother Lytton Strachey—both homosexual men—were the chief motors of their lives and the inspiration for their best work. Emily Carr was above all characterized by her relation to nature, the forests of western Canada and to the art of the First Nation tribes. If Claude Cahun's self-portraiture in her writings and photography, together with her lesbian lifestyle, seem miles apart from her later work with the Resistance on the island of Jersey, both kinds of experience define her eccentric being.

From my point of view, these were all formidable and courageous lives, resulting in formidable and courageous work. The struggle against what was accepted and against received wisdom nourished exactly that energy of emotion that characterized both the work and the life, one entwined with the other.

Bibliographies

Dorothy Bussy

Archives, *Bibliothèque nationale*. Dossier Roger Martin du Gard.
Bussy, Dorothy (as "Olivia"), *Olivia*. London: Grey Arrow, 1960.
Guerard, Albert J. *André Gide*. Cambridge: Harvard University Press, 1969.
Selected Letters of André Gide and Dorothy Bussy. ed. Richard Tedeschi, Oxford and New York: Oxford University Press, 1983.
Cahiers André Gide, no. 4: Les Cahiers de la Petite Dame: 1918–1929.
———. *Cahiers André Gide*, nos. 9–11. Correspondance André Gide — Dorothy Bussy, établie par Jean Lambert.
Sheridan, Alan. *André Gide: A Life in the Present*. Cambridge: Harvard University Press, 1999.

Claude Cahun (Lucie Renée Mathilde Schwob)

Claude Cahun, *Ecrits:* édition présentée et établie par François Leperlier. Paris: Jean-Michel Place, 2002. (E)
Claude Cahun Photographe, Exhibition Catalogue, Musée d' Art Moderne de la Ville de Paris. Paris: Jean-Michel Place, 1995.
Leperlier, François. *L'Ecart et la métamorphose*. Paris: Jean-Michel Place, 1992.
Krauss, Rosalind, "Claude Cahun and Dora Maar: By Way of Introduction," in *Bachelors*. Cambridge and London; MIT Press, 1999.
Monahan, Laurie, "Radical Transformations: Claude Cahun and the Masquerade of Womanliness" in *Inside the Visible: An Elliptical Traverse of 20th Century Art In, Of, and From the Feminine*. Cambridge and London: MIT Press, 1996.
Thyme, Lzzie, director: *Playing a Part: The story of Calude Cahun*, 2004

Emily Carr

The Complete Writings of Emily Carr. Vancouver/Toronto Douglas & McIntyre, 1997.
Carr, Emily. *The Book of Small*. Toronto: Irwin, 1942.
———. *Growing Pains: An Autobiography*. Toronto: Irwin, 1946.
———. *Hundreds and Thousands: The Journals of an Artist*. Toronto: Irwin publishers, 1966.

Blanchard, Paula. *The Life of Emily Carr*. Vancouver: Douglas and Macintyre, 1987.

Shadbolt, Doris. *The Art of Emily Carr*. Seattle: University of Washington Press, 1979.

The Sketchbooks of Emily Carr. Seven Journeys: Vancouver: Douglas and McIntyre, 2002.

The Emily Carr Omnibus. Seattle: University of Washington Press, Shadbolt preface, 1993.

Emily Carr Archives, Parnall Collection, Victoria, British Columbia. (1911–1930).

Carrington

Archives of the Harry Ransom Humanities Research Center, Austin, Texas (HRRC)

Carrington: Selected Letters & Extracts from her Diaires, ed. David Garnett. New York: Ballantine, 1974. (C)

Caws, Mary Ann. *Women of Bloomsbury: Virginia, Vanessa, Carrington*. New York and London: Rutledge, 1990.

———. *Carrington and Lytton: Alone Together*. London: Cecil Woolf, 1996.

———. and Sarah Bird Wright. *Bloomshbury and France*. New York: Oxford University Press, 2000.

Gerzina, Gretchen. *Carrington: A Life*. New York: Norton, 1989.

Hill, Jane. *The Art of Dora Carrington*. New York: Thames and Hudson, 1994.

Knapp, Bettina. *Judith Gautier: Writer, Orientalist, Musicologist, Feminist. A Literary Biography*. Dallas, TX: Hamilton Books, 1994.

Judith Gautier

Lanore, Fernand, et Sorlot, François. *La vie de Judith Gautier: Egerie de Victor Hugo et de Richard Wagner*: Ed. Fernand Lanore, Francois Sorlot, 1 rue Palatine, Paris 1990; 1996.

Richardson, Joanna. *Judith Gautier: A Biography*. London: Quartet Books Ltd, 1986. (JR)

Gautier, Judith as Judith Walter. *Le Livre de Jade*. Paris: Lemerre, 1867. Paris: Librairie Plon., Editions d'histoire et d'art, 1933. *Chinese Lyrics from the Book of Jade*. Translated from the French of Judith Gautier by James Whitall. Erskine McDonald, Ltd, 1919.

As Judith Mendès:

———. *Le Dragon Impérial*. Paris: Lemerre, 1869.

———. *L'Usurpateur*. Librairie Internationale. Albert Lacroix, 1875. Translated *La Soeur du Soleil*. Paris: 1897.

As Judith Gautier: *La Fille, du Ciel*. Paris: Translated as The Daughter of Heaven. Calman-Levy, 1911. (H)

Richard Wagner et son oeuvre poétique, depuis Rienzi jusqu'à Parsifal. Paris: Charaway frères, 1882.

La Conquête du paradis. Paris: Frinzine, 1887.

Parsifal. Traduction nouvelle s'adaptant à la musique. Paris: Société française d'éditions artistiques, 1898.

Le Collier des jours: souvenirs de ma vie. Paris: Felix Juven, 1902.

Le Second Rang du collier: souvenirs littéraires. Paris: Felix Juven, 1903.

Le Troisième Rang du collier. Felix Juven, 1909. (English version: *Wagner at Home.* Mills and Boon, 1910.)

Auprès de Richard Wagner: Souvenirs (1861–1882). Paris: Mercure de France, 1943.

Web page of Monsalvat for "Wagner's Muse" under http:home.c2i.net/monsalvat. htm (Monsalvat).

Sabor, Rudolph. Richard Wagner, *Der Ring des Nibelungen, a companion volume.* London and New York: Phaidon, 1997.

Paula Modersohn-Becker

Modersohn-Becker, Paula. *Letters and Journals*, ed. Gunter Busch and Liselotte von Reinken. New York: Taplinger, 1983. (M)

Perry, Gillian. *Paula Modersohn-Becker.* London: The Women's Press, 1979.

Rich, Adrienne, "Paula Becker to Clara Westhoff," in *The Vintage Book of Contemporary Cameron Poetry*, ed J.D. Mc Clatchy. New York: Vintage, 1990, pp. 367–369.

Rilke, Rainer Maria, "Requiem for a friend," in *The Selected Poetry of Rainer Maria Rilke*, ed. and tr. Stephen Mitchell. New York: Vintage, 1984, pp. 73–90.

Suzanne Valadon (Marie-Clémentine Valade)

Archives du Musée Nationale Moderne, Biblio the'que Kandinky (Fond Masle), Paris.

Suzanne Valadon, ed. Daniel Marchesseau. Martigny: Fondation Pierre Gianadda, 1996.

Carco, Francis. *L'Ami des peintres.* Paris: 1953.

Caws, Mary Ann. "Suzanne Valadon: Not Just His Mummie," in *Women Seeking Expression: France 1789–1914.* Ed. Rosemary Lloyd and Brian Nelson.

Jacomelti, Nesto. *Suzanne Valadon.* Geneva: Editions Pierre Cailler, 1947.

Jullian, Philippe. *Montmartre.* New York and Oxford: Oxford University Press, 1977.

Koren, Elaine Todd. *Suzanne: Of Love and Art.* New York: 2001.

Pétrides, Paul. *L'Oeuvre complète de Suzanne Valadon.* Paris: Compagnie Française des Arts Graphiques, 1971.

Peyramaure, Michel. *Les Escaliers de Montmartre; Le Temps des Ivresses: Suzanne Valadon: Roman*. Paris: Robert Laffont, 1998.

Rose, June. *Mistress of Montmartre: A Life of Suzanne Valadon*. London: Richard Cohen Books, 1998. (V)

Rosinsky, Thérèse Diamand. *Suzanne Valadon*. New York: Universe, 1994.

Storm, John. *The Valadon Drama*. New York: E.P. Dutton & Co, 1959.

Warnod, Jeanine. *Suzanne Valadon*. Translated by Shirley Jennings. Naefels, Switzerland: Bonfini Press Corp, 1981. New York: Crown Publishers, N.Y.

General

Barthes, Roland. *Camera Lucida*, trans. Richard Howard. London: Vintage, 1993.

Broude, Norma, and Mary D. Garrard. *The Expanding Discourse: Feminism and Art History*. Boulder, Colorado: Westview, 1992.

Caws, Mary Ann. *Sorrealist Painters and Poets*. Cambridge, Mass: MIT, 2000.

———. *Picasso's Weeping Women: The Life and Work of Dora Maar*. Boston: Little Brown, 2000.

Chadwick, Whitney. *Women, Art, and Society (World of Art)*. New York: Thames and Hudson, 2002.

Murat, Laure. *Passage de l'Odéon: Sylvia Beach, Adrienne Monnier et la vie littéraire à Paris dans l'entre-deux-guerres*. Paris: Arthème Fayard, 2003.

Nochlin, Linda. *Representing Women*. New York: Thames & Hudson, 2002.

———. *Women, Art, and Power*. New York: Harper and Row, 1988.

Parker, Rozsika and Pollock, Griselda. *Old Mistresses: Women, Art and Ideology*. London: Pandora/Routledge, 1981.

Sedgwick, Eve. *Epistemology in the Closet*. Harmondsworth, England: Penguin, 1990.

INDEX